How A Killer

Changed My Life:

A Story of A Little Life That Made A Big
Difference

A Little Dedication

By eleventh grade I had really become a much more manageable guy, so we won't talk about ninth or tenth grade so much. Maybe I thought I was going to stay a little tough, but that was before I met Ms. D. LaRouth Perry (now Dr. Perry), who I was blessed to have as my English teacher at Rogers High School in Toledo, Ohio.

Teaching was not a job for Dr. Perry—it was a purpose. She is designed for it. While many students that did not have the luck to be in her class simply came to school to pass another day, we came to learn, engage, and build another part of ourselves that would become a part of our story. And we did that while she encouraged, supported, and cheered us all the way.

Oh, yeah, she yelled at us, too. When we said, "I can't." See, Dr. Perry hates that phrase; maybe more than any other, I suppose. She showed us how to think beyond it, too. For that I simply say, "Thank you, Ms. P."

"Lend me your eyes,
I can change what you see."

~Mumford & Sons,
Awake My Soul, 2009

Prologue

I had lived a pretty happy life in Washington, D.C. for over twenty years, where I taught AP Chemistry for about fifteen years, got married, and remodeled some as we moved to three houses over that time for a few different reasons. Unfortunately, we got divorced, and now five years later I can make better sense of why about that and a lot of other things.

Over that time, I dated here-and-there (including two relationships of consequence), continued trying to make my claim at work for something more aligned with my goals (notwithstanding that, I very much love my work), and planned some pretty big ideas about next steps on all fronts. Family visited my new home in Florida, I went back home and visited back to D.C. from time-to-time to visit family and friends. I traveled a lot for work, often to new places that I was excited to visit.

At the same time, I became a little more reflective (as I suspect many of us do), and I started to piece together with the help of someone very special what to make important, turn my focus toward, and attend to if I were to make sense of what I've missed before and what I was ready to see moving forward. And that leads me to this story.

~

In the Broadway musical *Hamilton,* the final song contemplates whether our stories get told—and who will tell them. Well, I'm going to tell you hers. See, she never spoke a word but said a lot, and she never left the house but showed me the world. This is what I think she would want you to know.

1

Just a Little About Her

I suppose that it was possible to have a more suitable name for her, but because I didn't come up with it and she never acts on the expectations such a misfit name might imply, it sounded like a fine name. In fact, it's really an antonym to her life and personality because she indeed has a very different mindset than her name might cause one to think she should have. Even though Tubby, Fluffy, or even a mundane Slate would match her well, Killer is just her everyday name anyway. Besides, she appears to really like her name, or could I just clang a dinner plate on the counter while calling any name?

In T.S. Eliot's *Old Possum's Book of Practical Cats* we are reminded that cats have three names. Killer, then, is her *particular* name—the name that carries with it her confidence and prestige when she's among others. And she, of course, has a few *everyday* names, or nicknames, as well (including one that only I use): Killers with an *s* (although I am not sure that counts as an actual nickname), Girlie-girl, Baby doll (of course), Baby Killer, and some other standard-fare terms of endearment. As Eliot warns us, we'll never know what her *third* name is even though she's considering it all the time. We'll talk about that later. But, as it is, Killer is her name, and that sits with me just fine.

~

Killer is a girl. And she enjoys being a girl. I know this because she prefers fluffy beds, soft feathers, and other trappings that as best I can tell would suggest complete adoption of feline femininity. She also likes men. Not cats that are adult males but human men. I suspect this is because she very well knows how pretty she is, and she believes that it is an affront to the world if she fails to allow a member of the opposite sex a few moments to take her in. But it is worth noting that it is just a few moments—do not expect to dillydally with your admiration. A representative interaction should begin with an acknowledgement of her presence through a call for her (remember, she likes her name), a pause while she sniffs about your calf, and then a gentle permissive nudge that you may stroke along her back or scratch behind the ears. Then, it is over. As quickly as she has given you the honor, she moves beyond you; smoothly, as if being carried away in a palanquin adorned in velvet and gilded edges, which her demeanor might cause you to picture while you watch her stride away.

~

Her walk is slow and intentional, as if to announce and provide us a reminder of her existence rather than as transport to follow the path of daylight around the house—she is a bit of a mobile sundial. Of course, this is to ensure that a warmth soaks into her blueish-gray fur as she prepares for one of the several rehearsal naps leading to the matinee nap that occurs at some point in midafternoon when the sun lingers along the living room lanai doors for more than three hours. (It is then that her only boorish character shows: snoring.) Although she always requires the texture of a soft blanket for her overnight slumber, almost any surface is sufficient to bring on a nap. She particularly likes those curved cardboard scratchers, which can readily be prepared by an intense scratching and that soften over time to reveal the true shape that her Russian Blue fur conceals. An occasional glance with heavy eyelids toward a noise or a voice is all that one can expect during an afternoon nap, as there is not even a toy that causes her to deprive herself of the comfort of relaxing in the Florida sun.

When she does play from bed or otherwise, however, it appears assuredly an effort to entertain me rather than for her own enjoyment. Without rising, she obliges me with a half-hearted swipe at the advancing feather before contently watching it pass by her. As it disappears from view, she turns her glance away seemingly in hopes that the feather bird would find its way out of the house so she can return to whatever kind of seafood she had been dreaming about. Instead, though, it comes back at her, and she dutifully shows me how excited she is by swiping again with all the eagerness of someone gathering the supplies needed to clean a bathroom. Now, when she is up and about her enthusiasm is more obvious; but, nonetheless, while she enjoys catching the feather by mistake as she puts on her show, Killer is not tricked into thinking a feather on a string is going to be hunted and made into her next dish.

The laser light is altogether another story. The laser light is her favorite. On a scale, it is perhaps just above women, but absolutely below treats. When the laser darts from floor to wall, Killer crouches low behind the chair legs in the dining room that act as the sheltering blades of the grassland. The red dot–this understudy for the gazelle or wildebeest–has no chance of escape as she plans her attack. First, she follows it for a while to get a sense of how it moves across the imagined savannah. Then, she repositions herself so that little is between her and the prey–maybe just a table leg or an empty box that had once been her den. Finally, she sprints from her hiding place (that as you and I well know was never hiding her) and attacks the dot with both front paws, claws extended and her full body ready to push it into the vertical ground the wall simulates as she makes it surrender. But, despite her planning and agility, it gets away to the floor or onto the adjacent wall, and we start the hunt again.

We can only do this for about ten minutes because her heart races so fast I have always worried whether she was going to make it, and I've not been able to convince myself since that her heart should go so fast! No matter to her, she is satisfied at the exhibition of her skills in scaring the dot off somewhere, at least, and she believes all she needs is a good rest and she will get it next time.

~

As any cat owner knows, now that we have covered napping and hunting, there is really only one more important part of a cat's life: food (although this story is intended to show you another importance we might have overlooked). Killer is what we'd call a connoisseur. Not in the sense that we usually think of one being a connoisseur as it relates to food, such as one that can expertly distinguish a nuanced change in a taste or characterize the cooking technique of a lavish dish; see, that is a connoisseur of *food*. Killer is instead a connoisseur of *eating*. This is a different expertise and skill set altogether.

A feline expert in eating is adept at knowing that the butter has been taken from the refrigerator and is likely setting on the counter waiting for the toast to be ready. An expert in eating recognizes the sound of a foil lid being ripped from a yogurt cup even when napping. And an expert in eating knows exactly how to find the spoon rest used after her human makes poached chicken to ensure the drippings don't go to waste. Cottage cheese (large curd), Cheerios (but not the chocolate ones), and Pringles crumbs (importantly, only the original flavor) round out her time-to-time allowances of people food. Killer certainly lives up to the expectations she has set for herself in being such an expert. In fact, she is such an expert that she consistently scores in the mid-teens, and I am trying to bring that back down—eleven pounds would be nice.

~

I don't know much about Killer as a kitten; see, she was already eight or nine when I lucked out getting her in my life. I can imagine that her round, full face was just a smaller version of the one she has now—almost like a chipmunk, but with even bigger cheeks. And I would guess that she has been loaded with these tufts of color-changing fleecy fur since birth; hints of blue, gray, and umber appear throughout the day depending on the light that hits her. Her stubby legs strike you as too short for her body, but she manages well with them as they carry her around low to the ground and can readily get her into a trot when the moment calls for it. They are just tall enough to keep her little pouch from dragging on the floor, but they get her moving fast enough so that it swings just slightly back-and-forth like a woman's purse might as she walks briskly along the sidewalk.

But nothing catches your attention more than her looking directly at you. Her eyes are the most beautiful hues of green and blue that any cat has ever before displayed. Against a backdrop of the potted outdoor plants, her eyes match the blueish-green aloe vera stems, but while lounging by the pool, her eyes mirror the color of the water that outlines a Caribbean island where the water transitions from the deep sapphire blue of the Atlantic to the aquamarine along the edges of the beaches. They can be spellbinding, if for no other reason than to acknowledge a small beauty provided us in the world that we should notice.

Killer had a few homes as a kitten and young cat. It was in these earlier homes that she formed an affection for dogs–well, an affection for hissing at them. While she never takes any more substantive steps at expressing her displeasure beyond that and a few swipes for no reason, Killer has always been an independent woman that is much more comfortable in the presence of her human (with an emphasis on *man*, recall) than other four-legged beings.

~

Purring is a regular part of Killer's day, and she is fond to purr alone lying in the sun or waiting in anticipation for a breakfast or dinner serving. Even as she walks from one room to another she can be heard droning a gentle hum. She purrs often enough that I think of how my grandma used to walk around the house humming–kind of like that self-assuring assertion that everything was good in her life. It comforted me to hear her doing that; in a sometimes empty, quiet house Killer's melodies seem to make it brighter and filled.

Killer enjoys being near me. She likes to follow me up in the morning, and, as many cats must, believes that the morning bathroom stop for me is intended only to give her some petting and scratching. In fact, I might have more pictures of Killer looking up at me with my feet on either side of her than I care to admit to, and I certainly have more than I care to admit to the truth about their location! For her, it is a few moments when she rubs against my leg and returns the affection I show her as best she can.

~

Bedtime is a special time with her because she carries out a routine that cannot change or she vocalizes disapproval. And, by vocalized, I mean I will say *"ouch"* as she scratches her way to where she intends herself to be. Killer spends a good amount of time planning her high jump onto the bed, where her pill-covered blanket is waiting. With precision like both a surveyor and a fighter pilot, she evaluates angles, tangents, and trajectories that will land her right where she can see, as if she forgets and fears what is beyond the visible horizon from night-to-night. Once her geometry and calculations are complete and she paces side-to-side for a final assessment, she springs from the floor and lands exactly where she expects, curling up with a purr and a slightly demanding nudge that petting should commence.

I never object to petting her. While I talked about her color, let me take a minute for you to realize her texture. Her fur is soft like those faux bear rugs all of us rub at IKEA but that I'm not sure many people really buy—you know the one: "Honey, feel this; isn't it soft?" That one is Killer fur. Thick and soft as it envelopes every finger as each disappears into it. If we lived in a cold climate, she would be the even *more* perfect nighttime companion.

~

Killer is about fourteen now—so, she's a graceful senior in human years. She hasn't changed much in the five years she's been with me, except that she seems to view herself as more of a glamourous diva now than then. Good for her.

And with that we have a pretty complete introduction to our main character. Well, except for all the rest she wants you to think about.

2

Prelude to Some Lessons

We had just moved to Florida, and Killer did great on the fourteen-hour trip. Of course, unlike with a dog, we did not need to stop because her living room, bedroom, and bathroom were all well-appointed and accommodated within the cab of the Tacoma. The only stops were for me and at the usual times she expected to eat, which happen to be at eight in the morning and five in the evening.

On the trip, Killer at various times slept on the passenger seat, the back seat floor, or on my lap. It annoyed her to no small degree that she could not see out of the windows very well, so she tried frequently to stand on my thighs and place her front paws on the steering wheel, which gave her at least a little crescent view out the windshield. However, it was always short-lived because I needed to shoo her back to lying down when I needed to take a sharper curve (which is a welcome driver engagement on the otherwise loathsome length of Interstate 95 from Washington, D.C. to Jacksonville, Florida). Once she sensed that we were back on the straightaways, she would crawl back into that position, which reminded me of that a perpetrator who is now in frisking position might take along a dark alley's brick wall in some C.S.I. episode.

~

When we arrived at the new house, she spent plenty of time looking around, finding the new corners where she could nap or groom, and taking in the smells of my aunt's dog that had lived there before us—often looking abruptly at a noise to confirm it was not him still here. I, on the other hand, was exhausted and ready to go to bed—how lucky to be a cat and never be asked to take over the driving!

We spent the first night in the house in what would later be the guest bedroom. It has a nice Murphy bed, and the king-sized sheets I was able to find draped over the queen-sized mattress just enough for Killer to hide behind them underneath the bed and hunt my toes as I finished getting the bed ready. By the time the last pillow was thrown on the bed, Killer finally tired of her assault, and she hopped up into bed (after the mathematical evaluations were completed) to sleep for the night. And thus started our bedtime routine moving forward; although, the toe attacks faded as she got older.

The next day, I started the job of unpacking and arranging the new house. Of course, task one was to find her beds, toys, and water fountain, as she was no longer accustomed to still water. I had read that cats prefer moving water because they are leery of standing water—apparently they sense that it might not be clean. So I bought her the fountain: stainless at the bottom but with a pink plate covering the top and a purple flower-shaped spout that spilled water for her in five directions.

It is fun to watch her drink from it. She approaches it with some skepticism even if it is the fifth trip of the day and twists and darts her head trying to plan for the best direction from which to approach it. The first and second attempts usually land as a noseful of water and twitching whiskers, and she shrinks back–often looking around as if to see if anyone has noticed (I look away out of respect). By the third try, she usually starts feeling the water on her tongue after a few tentative slurps; she is full into the fountain until quenched.

At any rate, by mid-morning all her things were placed about the house, and she not surprisingly spent the rest of the morning ignoring them to investigate, rest in, and rub against the boxes that just hours ago held said things.

By early afternoon, I was ready for a nap, and by now rugs started to brighten the rooms, furniture began to define the spaces, and knick-knacks and lamps started dotting the landscape of end tables, nightstands, and small shelving units. However, I really wanted to finish, so I continued opening the various boxes marked "LR," "Guest," and "Bath" until late into the afternoon. Killer reacted to each new thing that appeared with a typical curiousness.

Once she confirmed for herself that an object was something she had previously known, she checked out the next item until she reached the same conclusion, and this continued as I worked nonstop. I was off for the next few days, so I did ask myself more than once why I didn't take a little break, which Killer was apt to do without notice.

Because this was my aunt's old house, I had already built a large bookcase into the corner of the old formal dining room in preparation for moving. This was a good idea, as more than 300 books had also made the trip to Florida from D.C. And it was these to which Killer and I needed to turn our attention. Me so that I could get a feeling of a bunch unloaded quickly, and her because I think she knew at least twenty boxes were about to be emptied into a makeshift condominium fort across the living room floor. I lugged them into place near the bookshelf, and Killer and I both grabbed a bit of water before digging in.

Like most cats, Killer loves boxes, and she has a special place in her heart for a specific box I'll tell you about later. You can imagine, then, that this move made her very happy as she scurried across the floor to run from one to another. Once inside, she crouched low as if to conceal herself from the wilderness outside and then lunged at the right moment when a flap of an adjacent box moved when the ceiling fan's currents hit it just right.

~

Brené Brown had published the *Atlas of the Heart* just about at the same time I was moving south—and moving on from a couple-year relationship after my divorce. I had purchased it for us, thinking it might have been a great resource for both of us to learn more about how we think, feel, understand, and respond to ourselves, each other, and the world. Of course, it didn't quite result in that as I don't think we ever opened it; but now here was this book right on top of the first box that I opened.

Let me say first, if you haven't seen the book, it's gorgeous. The stars of the night sky surround the smallest flowers that we might not even take note of as we pass them on the sidewalk, all of which are wrapped into a profile of a heart printed on a bold red slipcover. It is organized unit-like by the emotions we feel when experiences of the world cause certain responses, such as happiness, confusion or hurt. Initially, one might even think it almost encyclopedic when it's browsed on the shelf, but I hope anyone that has done so looked further.

Now that I have read it through (I intentionally did not say *finished* it—I'm not sure I'll ever put it away), I can reflect more meaningfully to briefly describe it than I could have that night. In contrast to simple entries about our emotions, our responses to them, and the ways in which they shape our next steps—or the ways in which *we shape them with our next steps*—it is a story of who we are, and how we can use who we are to connect with ourselves and others. The book is a journey rather than just a book to be read and marked complete. The interesting part is that it feels like a different journey every time you sit to reread some of it—its meaning affected by your current feelings—and I have read it a lot since I opened that box. (I hope Ms. Brown does not take exception to my description!)

By now it had grown dark, as it was nearing winter and shorter days were already here. So, I turned on a light and took another look at the cover of this book while Killer rested alongside. And right there in plain words is what I had not understood to be the truth of the matter: *We are the mapmakers and the travelers!* We're not just the ones that chart the courses we follow *or* the ones that follow determined paths, but instead, we do both. How had I not yet learned that better?

~

Well, I'm glad I have Killer—she helps me to see the better paths and to create new ones.

3

Lesson One: Taking Chances

Winters in Florida are not that difficult. Well, the winters in *southern* Florida are not that bad–I've heard a story or two about cold and snow not being uncommon up in the panhandle, which is why Killer and I were south of Sarasota in North Port. Had my aunt and uncle bought a home much farther north, I would certainly have reconsidered buying it from them when they decided that it was outsized for them as they got older.

North Port is a fine enough place to settle–my only real needs from a geography perspective were warm weather and an airport, as I traveled for work a lot. Killer didn't mention any specific needs when I told her we were moving, and I am sure she approves of my choice. It turns out Killer never made too much fuss about decisions I made unless they affected her mealtimes.

The house is on a circle, which means there is no through traffic, and the early residents on the street bought up all the lots to turn a planned nine houses on the street to just three. It is farthest back on the circle, too, outlined along the back by old palm trees and one of the many canals that serve to manage waterflow in southwest Florida. The canal behind the house leads to another, larger canal, from which you can navigate all the way to Charlotte Harbor via the Myakka River on a small canoe or kayak until you reach the Gulf of Mexico. I have not traveled that far yet because there is a really low bridge that I'm still nervous about going under!

On one side, the yard opens to a few empty wooded lots, while on the other the neighbors' dogs fill their yards with the protective barks of two dogs who don't really know that the cars and people on the street all belong there (and bring them treats, too). On the same side are two looming southern live oak trees (*Quercus virginiana*, for those who might be interested). One has taken on a tall and lean approach to growing over its decades of life, while the other decided to branch about thirty feet from the ground and create an umbrella that extends to over twenty feet from the trunk all around. Their claim to fame is the thousands of leaves that flutter to the ground, blow across the roof, and fill the gutters throughout the year. Otherwise, they serve to nest some birds, provide some shade, and line a path back to the pool if you choose to walk around that way.

The front yard itself has only a single, short, kind of dilapidated tree in the center, but the immediate areas on either side of the walk extending up from the driveway contain just the right mix of small palm trees, flowers, and mounding grasses that lizards, bees, butterflies, and the seasonal brood of crickets find appealing and homey enough. From the big front window, Killer enjoys watching their family life as they move from plant to plant, tend to their routine, and leap for smaller insects that fall lower on the food chain. The front yard is also where the sun starts its day before it marches around toward the back of the house by late morning.

~

By late spring, I had grown accustomed to Killer using the window for some of her entertainment needs. She is fond of watching the lizards on the screens as they scurry about doing whatever it is that small lizards do when they go from the ground to the top of a screen! Until she has to chase the sun elsewhere or I leave for too long to another room, the small benches I placed there and the windowsill let her take her stationary nature walks and is where she is likely to be found until afternoon.

Her tail rests or moves with variable turns and cadence as creatures travel throughout the garden, and over time I started to think that I had decoded the messaging. A simple dangling downward toward the floor means that she has no interest in whatever is moving around out there. Slow thumping or swishing, though, means that she has some interest, but it is not likely to result in anything more than a rather nonthreatening glance through the window. Once she progresses to tail flicking, however, her eyes widen, a slight growl rolls up from her throat, and you can see her rearranging herself as if to strike if this garden resident comes closer. But she never really rises from her restful position on the sill or bench; instead, she just responds with these small indicators that things have her attention.

~

I had not considered that she would want to go outdoors, and every time I thought about it I was apprehensive or just plain scared. By now Killer was my best companion, and I can't imagine a bobcat or an alligator dragging her off while I was helpless to rescue her! She has always been an indoor cat, and I figured that it is really what she likes, as she never gives much fuss when I go outside but she doesn't. She watches me work out there just the same as she does the other garden-dwellers—maybe she even thinks I am hunting something for her, as she always meets me at the door when I return.

~

It started small by holding her in my arms and walking along the walk to the driveway with her when I first decided to try letting Killer get a little closer to those gardens she had been watching since last winter. She purred and darted her eyes toward the same little moving things she saw now from my arms that before were separated by the glass she sometimes bumped against when standing her ground. I was still nervous, but her excitement was about equal to what I see when she hunts the red laser prey.

A few days later, I set her down on the walk—I didn't stand fully upright for the next thirty minutes so that I could keep my hands about an inch from her in case she took off. So, there I was, just a comma-shaped figure who looked like he was struggling to get his cat in his reach. (I'm glad there's only one neighbor that can really see me there.) But, over the next several days, I grew more comfortable to watch her from just a short distance, and then farther, until over time I would even let her out while I was at my desk and could see her through the window she used to spy behind.

And here's what I see: absolute joy. She is not afraid (as I had been about her going out there), and she does not want to go very far from the house. What she does want to do is to chase a grasshopper from the lilac bush to the base of the palm tree and then be distracted by a lizard that sees her coming but slithers away to avoid her pounce. She wants to paw at a stalk of grass that has gone to seed and waves to her in the wind like a play date that just noticed his friend made it to the playground. I see her simply enjoying the things that to her before were just scentless imaginings through a window.

She rolls on the warm driveway to scratch herself and leave her scent wherever she can, and she lurks low behind the potted plants when someone from the neighborhood chooses *her* street as their dog-walking trail. She watches the herons go by on their way to the canal behind the house, picking as they do at the insects from the yard, but she surely knows that those beaks have a much longer reach than the claws of her stubby legs! She even safely lets the rabbits run through the yard without giving chase, although all systems are poised to go—tail, ears, eyes, stance—if they come just close enough.

As summer ended, I watched Killer experiencing new things in her life that she had not seen before, at least not seen close enough to also smell and feel. She crunched on little leaves under the southern live oaks you read about earlier and even made her way to the end of the driveway to get a better view of the barking dogs protecting no one from nothing–but still practicing in case the need ever arrived. She traded the sun coming in through the window for the real feel of the sun on her skin, and she soaked it in as she fell asleep on the walk.

~

We grow content to look through fictional windows all the time. How often has any one of us just watched without acting and missed the set of experiences on the other side? As I watched Killer in the garden, I wondered if I had too often.

~

When I was in middle school and high school I used to be jealous of my friends that were good at a variety of things: playing instruments, sports, or even acting in school plays. (Turns out, I was kind of envious of the kids I taught for all the same reasons sometimes, too.) Back then, I was afraid to try stuff that I wasn't sure I would be good at. So now, I don't play an instrument, I can maybe get through a softball game at least without embarrassing myself, and the only acting I can do is the drama I show when I can't find Killer because she has hidden herself in a cabinet again.

I don't much believe in such a notion as fear of failure anymore. Instead, I think that I have looked through the glass too long on things simply because I didn't get up and do something! It's so easy to let a great idea slip away or a dream go unrealized because we let other things—often, not even important things—get in the way. Or worse, excuses for why *not* to do something take over.

~

My grandfather built houses in Mansfield, Ohio during the 1940s and 1950s. My mom's earliest memories were of helping to put the roof on the house in which she and her two sisters and one brother grew up. (Now that I think about it, I realize she must have been about only 7 or 8, so I am not sure that was a great idea.) The neighborhood in which they lived was almost entirely houses built by my grandfather, and I guess some child labor for the roofing.

His more-distant relatives and his grandparents, aunts and uncles, and parents had come to the United States from present-day Austria starting in the 1860s through the early part of the twentieth century. His was the first generation to be born in the United States in the family. In Austria, many of his family members were engaged in the woodworking or building fields, and the records of their fields (or *callings* on the ships' manifests) can be found in the Ellis Island records as well as period U.S. census records:

> *Jacob, 1868, carpenter*
> *Nikolas, 1893, carpenter*
> *Josef, 1902, laborer*

About fifteen family members came to the U.S. during that time, and they were able to bring only a few items with them. Many of the women, including my great-grandmother, favored sentimental items, such as the seventeenth-century dessert glass set I have now on a shelf in my dining room. Men, however, needed to bring items that supported their work or trade, and family still have some of the items they brought, including a bench lathe brought over by Nikolas, who was my grandfather's dad, and an old folding wooden measuring tape, which I am lucky to have now.

It made sense with all the knowledge and skill brought by these folks that my grandfather took up building with wood. He started with tables, chairs, and household items to learn the craft at its most fine level, and only later did he turn toward the larger-scale building-type work. This let him learn the intricacies of creating moldings and other decorative elements that the finishing of his houses required.

My grandfather built everyday houses— not mansions or elaborate estates. Most of the homes he constructed were probably about fifteen hundred square feet. The baby boom of the mid-to-late 1940s gave him plenty of work, as new families and growing families moved from smaller homes into the developing areas outside of downtown. And while the homes were modest, his millwork was intricate but not extravagant. He outlined the windows with curved and scrolled moldings to add a touch of elegance to a living room or main bedroom. He carefully trimmed the front porch and roof gables with molding to add an air of sophistication to otherwise commonplace Mansfield post-war houses. Those houses are still there on Massa Avenue in Mansfield, while his brothers built in Ashland a few miles away.

~

As a teenager, I was always in awe of his garage workshop and all its tools, gadgets, and rows and rows of wood of every type (it was probably more than a garage, but that is what he called it). One thing I remember above anything else was the scent: fresh-cut wood and its shavings, and the smell of the short pieces being burned in the fireplace. I spent several summers with him trying to learn the same skills that he developed with his dad and uncles almost fifty years earlier and that had been part of the family for over one hundred. I enjoyed the summers, the time with him, and what I'll call the training, but I returned to a suburban home just before school was to start each fall with just a little garage and no real resources to duplicate what I had learned. But I thought of what I could do often.

Thirty years had intervened between those visits and the time I bought my house in Alexandria. My grandfather died in 2000, and he had asked often what my first project was going to be. I don't know what I told him anymore, but I know he would have liked to see it. I always had a reason that *it* wasn't ready: I didn't have the right tools, I needed to practice first before I tried it, or I just needed more time. Thirty years should have been enough.

~

I met my neighbor Nina even before I bought the house in Alexandria, Virginia in 2015. I noticed the beautiful mosaics hanging on her gate and along the front of her house when I was first looking with a real estate agent at the house next door to hers in which I had an interest. Each mosaic was made of thousands of small, hand-nipped, glimmering pieces of glass, and the sun caught them to make them shimmer even more brightly (although had the sun not shone on them they would have been just as gorgeous).

Nina is an artist of photography and mosaic work. She had a studio in Old Town Alexandria for many years, where she has become renowned for her photographic perspectives: Black church communities, women, and Alexandria history. Nature, too, is a favorite of hers, and many of her photographs later become the mosaics that now form the gallery passersby enjoy from the sidewalk.

I spent a lot of Sunday mornings with Nina in her backyard garden during the five years I lived next door, where we talked about a lot of things over the years. When we first met, she told me a lot about the plants and the trees in her back yard. It's an oasis of birds, butterflies, and insects surrounded by a lot of grassed-over, fenced-in lots. You can hear the babbling of a few ponds as the water runs into the basins, and the soft humming of the birdbath is only interrupted by quick flutters of a bird drying off after landing.

On one Sunday morning shortly after I sold the house, I shared with her that I wish I had a talent of sorts to share with the world when we were talking about her next project. Of course, she knew that I made little things from time-to-time, but I had not really dived into what I really wanted to do: make furniture using what my grandfather had shown me all those years ago.

In my home, I have the octagon table he made for that house on Massa Avenue, which fit perfectly into the L-shaped, cushioned bench seating he built against the wall to maximize space. (When I was younger, I pretended with my siblings and cousins that we were at a restaurant because of that bench seating, which squealed slowly when you sat down.) My mom has a small side table he made as one of his first projects, and its twin is with my aunt in Florida. The case of a grandfather clock is perhaps among his most detailed pieces, and that clock—now just entering its sixtieth year—is still announcing the time every fifteen minutes in the corner of my bedroom.

Nina and I talked about those furniture pieces that morning—I suppose they came up because I had already started to pack up the house, including the eight-sided table (which is what I still call it because when I first saw it as a toddler I didn't know it was an octagon!). We also talked about how I was looking for that spark to maybe explore creating art like she does, but that I had not found something I did well enough—or even really tried! She told me almost tersely when she said it (she is from Brooklyn), and it hit me just as sharply. I'll paraphrase, "You're already an artist—your medium is wood, and what you can make is just as beautiful as any painting, mosaic, poem, or music."

~

Sure, I had dabbled in a few things: an arbor for the backyard, rough-type building when I remodeled, and some picture framing. But I had not much explored anything more intricate beyond some shelving I created with some fun brackets I designed. They were nice, but I wasn't thinking of them as art, for sure!

Shortly after I breathed deeply and let Killer outside, I thought about that backyard conversation. As I saw Killer enjoying the outdoors, I thought that my wait could now easily become forty years if I allowed it to be.

Since that recollection almost four years ago, I have refined my craft in building dining and coffee tables with new and unusual designs to fit different styles, used interesting wood combinations to add interest and character, and tried out new approaches to staining and painting that give a unique look to a piece. I have tried exotic woods and everyday woods, traditional methods of joinery and ways that add to the aesthetic to complement a decor, and I've just started to try some novel applications of inlays and edge designs. Today, I look at these pieces at my home and in the homes of others where they've landed—I really do see the art in them.

I recall this story because for thirty years we can look through our *own* old dining room windows—failing to notice that experiences are there for the taking if we don't become spectators.

~

I had been an observer and an audience to other peoples' art in all its forms. Now, here it was that Killer's move from behind the glass let me see mine, too.

4

Lesson Two: Mindfulness

The small tree in the front yard had now become Killer's throne area from which she reviewed her kingdom of about three-quarters of an acre. That tree provides her a little shade right in the middle of it all and gives her some time to watch squirrels in addition to her usual companions. She is not allowed along the back by the canal and the final quarter acre—royal audiences with her subjects back there are only through the lanai screen because alligators are bigger. With teeth.

Speaking of the lanai, when she is out there she is a lot more active in chasing lizards, often bringing them into the living room or bedroom to share with me. I read that this is an honor of sorts when cats do this, but I find it to be kind of gross to watch her coming toward me with just a little tail hanging out of one side of her mouth and little petrified eyes out of the other. Nonetheless, she presents these trophies to illustrate her prowess as a hunter and to offer me some of her reptilian spoils. More often than not, once she loses interest in batting it around, it still has enough life that I scoop it up and toss it out the front door.

The lanai is also usually the evening location. Made of concrete, it warms nicely throughout the day, but it does not surrender its heat after the sun sets. So, the lanai gives Killer a good place to splay out on her back and roll around when she can no longer go out front after dark. She never lands in the pool, although she will quickly jump back when she notices she is much closer than expected as she completes a roll—a surprised look on her face as if she had never known it was there. But I know she does— she has developed a particular relationship with the pool where she hunches close to ball-shaped and just dips her face into it to get a drink as if it is some kind of large water bowl I put out there for her.

~

By late September in our second year at the house, we were starting to get a sense that a hurricane was on its way. Hurricane Charley hit the house with his northern periphery in 2004. Compared to the devastation to Punta Gorda and other areas to the south, North Port fared pretty well, and the house only needed some soffit panels replaced and a repositioning of the shed, which had been reoriented about thirty degrees. I helped my aunt and uncle once everything reopened, and no other hurricane shook up the house since.

Even though I know I live in the center of the action for hurricanes, I had only just begun to create lists of things I should do to prepare (like learn how to use the generator) by late that summer. I had already prepared a "to-go" kit in case Killer and I had to evacuate, which held everything she needed and maybe something for me tucked in any available excess space. I had eight cans of wet food, a small seven-pound bag of dry food, one box of Churu (her absolute favorite), a feather toy, a small bag of catnip (and the fillable mouse toy), food and water bowls, one box of lightweight litter, and a travel litter box. I would grab her brush, the laser light, and a cardboard scratcher when the time came. A duplicate of her favorite blanket was in the kit, as well, but I suspect that she would know it was an imposter, so I made a note to try to remember the real one. She is not fond of the crate, but everything she needed was housed in it and ready to go, and I would replace those things with her when needed.

On September 23, forecasts put then-tropical storm Ian's track, who was named on the same day, far north of us into the panhandle of Florida some days later. Even as some computer models showed a much more southerly track, as late as September 27 the track was still sparing us. Ian threw a wrench into that by turning at the last minute, and on September 28 struck Florida just south of Punta Gorda, which is about twenty miles south of the house, before following almost the same track as Charley eighteen years before. The difference? Size and speed. Ian was huge, and he moved as sloth-like as his huge size might suggest he was able. Over the next twenty-four hours, the house got over twenty inches of rain, and it flooded as the canal systems were overwhelmed by the amount of water that Ian brought with him.

~

Killer and I had left for Miami the day before, and we were under a blanket together the next morning when the news reports announced the unexpected strength Ian had reached and the size to which he had grown. In fact, he continued to intensify even after landfall. We spent a couple days and nights there, and we planned on going home the next morning.

Killer adapted well to the confines of the Hilton Garden Inn near Miami International Airport. She didn't act weird about being someplace new, which was a relief for me, and I was glad that much of my unease was not picked up by her (as far as I could tell). She napped, snacked, and played just as normally as when at home. Her window view was a little higher, and she pretended to watch the planes land with me while I had my morning coffee and watched news reports from the west coast.

(Now, for those of you that don't know, it is important to note that it's not really the "*west coast*." Each coast*line* of Florida has a name, like the *Space Coast* of Cape Canaveral and the *Nature Coast* of the big bend with its untamed regions. We lived on the *Cultural Coast,* which is so named because of its attraction for musicians and artists and the presence of museums, such as the Ringling Museum, which should not be missed if you visit the area.)

We watched alternately the Weather Channel and local Tampa and Ft. Myers stations throughout the day. Killer got a couple of opportunities to run the hall, where she was very receptive to the scratches and rubs of some other folks sitting out the storm over on the *Gold Coast.*

I would like to think that I was calm and relaxed; but, of course, I was very anxious about the house and what we might do if it had sustained a lot of damage. I worked very hard to settle into this house and make it ours, and I feared that a lot of it would be gone based on video starting to trickle in by evening. To say that I felt overwhelmed would have understated it. Perhaps had I had someone to share it with I could have calmed a bit, but it was a lot to take in, and I felt quite helpless during that stay.

Phone calls to my dad and sister had a relaxing effect.

As I mentioned, Killer appeared to barely take notice that things were unusual. Sure, she knew there was no lanai and no tree in the middle of the yard, but she otherwise still hopped into bed on time, visited the scratching pad, and spent time on her back with the feather to entertain me. She grew especially partial to going behind the night stands to get into the drawers, which often sent me into a frenzy to find her. On the trip home—although it was really a few trips back because we could not get to the house on the first two tries—Killer traveled in style on the top of the crate in the passenger seat, loafing as a cat would and watching the limited view along Alligator Alley. She always acted surprised when a car came up on her right side, and she turned her head to watch it pass, glancing at it one final time before returning her attention to reviewing the more global scene available through the full-windshield view she had.

Although I wanted to believe the best and the house was fine, we were going to arrive back to no problem, and that no significant damage had occurred, I could not move my mind from the some of the videos I had already seen of North Port, Port Charlotte, and Punta Gorda. The flooding was record-breaking, and it stretched for miles down the coast toward Naples as well as inland beyond expectations. We were now approaching southwest Florida, and we would be home soon.

I looked over at Killer. She was now fighting sleep even while monitoring those passing homebound cars that kept popping into view. She had been so relaxed through the experience, and I considered a bit about how she just lets go and observes and takes in her new experiences. She clearly has it figured out because I could see that she was just enjoying the ride, and I wondered what it would take to do the same.

~

What I thought just then was how often did I live in the present and take the time to enjoy a moment. Did I often lose a memory before it could be created?

~

I am very happy to be older. I remember easily the times we went out to dinner as a family and had conversation and enjoyed the company of mom, dad, and the three of us (I have one older sister and one younger brother). There were no distractions of iPhones, notifications from watches, or tablets placed in front of us to "keep us busy" while we had dinner as a family. Instead, we acknowledged one another throughout the meals, we focused on what another talked about, and we appreciated that we had an opportunity to be together.

But I hardly write this to rail against technology that at the same time makes life easier, gives us access to things that used to be harder to get, and keeps folks together in ways that can even connect people separated by distance (and that I probably spend too much time on, myself). But that's not really the source of *my* failure to connect with a moment, anyway. Instead, what Killer showed me was that even in the ordinary there is a richness for experience and learning.

~

Killer takes in everything. As a cat, she has eyes that rival telescopes it seems, and she notices the smallest insects dancing around the porch lights after sunset. She darts her eyes between the three that illuminate the driveway so that she might get a glimpse of a dragonfly or a crane fly—for these she leaps forward for a closer view. This is her version of Cirque du Soliel—watching the twirls, spins, and twists of the participating acrobats. Sometimes the flurry at the streetlamp farther away catches her attention, too—what a show that provides! At the start of the day, she momentarily suspends eating her breakfast when she hears the alligators in the canal call out during May and June when they're looking for partners—she throws a glance to the dining room window to be sure that it isn't as near as it sounds. She might even just leap from the counter to the table to see if she can finally get a view of whatever it is that is again creating this deep rumble across the still dew-covered grass. And, throughout the afternoon she keeps track of every bird that lands on the blooms of flowers in the spring and summer around the front of the house—acknowledging each one as it flutters from stem to stem, giving each a second look even as the afternoon sun makes her squint as she lies there and discovers who stopped by to say hi.

Now, of course I know that this is not the same kind of interest that we might have in seeing the same things around us—some of this is for her just instinctive hunting and protection. However, when I watch her, I wonder if it's not in many ways her just taking an occasion to watch something new (or old), smell a new scent, or note the color of the feathers that land before her to be viewed. Nonetheless, like the calmness she showed enjoying the trip back after the hurricane, it makes me wonder how much is going on around me that I even fail to take notice of while she catches and senses every whisper of life around her.

~

Being present requires the same kind of observational pause of life that Killer does so effortlessly: it's really a *mindfulness* of the worlds in which we live—and not just the physical like I just shared about Killer but also the emotional that we share with ourselves and others. Mindfulness, then, takes on so many meanings: awareness of a moment while taking a walk, focusing on even just a quick conversation in the grocery store, taking the time to listen and respond to a loved one's need, or letting go of a real or self-imposed guilt that has weighted you down. I think of mindfulness as *interacting with a moment to give it meaning and understand its value.*

~

I carefully planned where along the bank of the canal tracing the outline of the back of my property I was going to remove some trees, wildflowers, and shrubs to clear an opening just wide enough so I could see any hiding alligators when slipping my kayak into the water. While the neighbors had removed most of the longstanding wild growth where their properties curved along the canal, I enjoyed both the natural appearance and the privacy that the growth afforded me. There are a dozen or so each of date palms, majesty palms, and royal palms out there (and a few that grow a lot closer to the ground), and each gives its own little character. As the sun sets, they offer a silhouette skyline against an orange-red sky that conjures up the text *FLORIDA* across it in those big, puffy, cartoon letters of a post card.

I selected the space I was going to clear so that it would result in minimal disruption to both the view from the house as well as to the preserve-like look that the whole backyard perimeter provided. Early one Saturday, then, I collected the tools I needed, and I started with the weeds and other less-than-pretty stuff that stood between the backyard grass line and the canal.

Most of the weeds seemed to continue for miles. They wound their way around nearby trees, coursed back on themselves, and extended outward from their roots in all directions. I had visions of both *Jurassic Park* and *Indiana Jones* running through my head as I sickled, shoveled, and clipped my way back toward the canal in what felt like just a few inches at a time. Soon, however, I was back to the bigger trees that grew not too far from the canal's edge. Which of these was going to go was my next decision. But then I looked up.

With bright pink, purple, blue, and white, the orchids revealed themselves as they now gleamed in full view of the sun just coming over the tops of the trees and down through their fronds onto their previously-shaded trunks. Each orchid petal soaked it in while reflecting their appreciation back as vivid display of color. So, as Killer showed me to do, I paused to give it meaning and value. To me, these were bunches of color that gift-wrapped the trees; to birds, these held morning meals; and to the trees, a responsibility to support. How lucky was I to have these in front of me.

So, I made my decision, and today I still walk past them with my kayak on my way to the neighbor's house to get into the canal.

~

I think of mindfulness, too, beyond the natural world that Killer admires so often to include, of course, exhibitions of empathy, acceptance, gratitude, and compassion in relationships. All of these require the two things that I claim define mindfulness: meaning and value—it's a thoughtful acknowledgement of someone else's viewpoints, needs, or choices followed by a response that does not judge, diminish, or dismiss. In fact, it's a lot of that stuff that we used to see that is now missing from what we understood to be healthy social engagement. And it's especially important in more intimate relationships—colleagues at work, our neighbors, and our most significant personal relationships. Let me talk about one that I've spent a lot of time thinking about.

Not that long ago, I was having a conversation (*maybe* a little argument) with someone who I started chatting with a little over two years ago. I think we're dating now, but it's over a long distance, so it's harder than I thought it would be. We visited my mom late last summer, and he seemed very distant and almost cold just sitting on the couch with barely a word except to answer questions, which I took as rude and not what I had expected to see as the first introduction to my mom.

Not having considered mindfulness so well yet, I became upset and frustrated. See, what I did was assign my own meaning to what I observed instead of finding out what was going on. Turns out, he's very shy, and when he meets new people, he recalls a history that reminds him of others not being so nice—picking on him or making fun of him for being different than them. I didn't know how present this memory still was for him day-to-day, and my reaction made him believe that I didn't value the experiences he still carries with him into every new social situation.

Here, a true mindfulness would have been for me to simply engage with my mom, encourage opportunities for him to share with us as he wanted, and accept without a word that it was as uncomfortable for him in this new situation in a lot of ways as the playground felt twenty years earlier. The empathy I could have shown would have shown I understand the meaning of his apparent detachment and would made him see that I value his experiences, needs, and struggles.

I will do better.

~

And mindfulness is important in one other relationship: the one we have with ourselves. Taking time to relax, to process a day's worth of experiences, or to consider how to move on from mistakes. It's an opportunity to be alone with our thoughts. Killer does that.

Killer likes to spend time alone in her corner bed from time-to-time. She doesn't want a lot of attention there; instead, it's her place to go when she just watches what's going on in the parts of the house that she can see from that spot behind my desk. She takes note of the kittens moving about and exploring the reaches of the room for the small hair piles that the fan carries around the room and gently lies down near the baseboards. She glances over at the windchimes that hang by the door to my room, and she tends to a little grooming here-and-there as she simply takes a little time to herself.

~

For us, mindfulness is not so easy—that's because for us it needs to be intentional.

5

Lesson Three: Patience & Tolerance

By later in the winter following Ian, the house had come back together nicely; in fact, it was now becoming the house that I had wanted all along: my choice of new cabinets in the kitchen, new bamboo floors to replace the carpet, and a new dark green exterior so that it would better just blend into the background of the trees.

Shortly after everything was mostly put back together (I am notorious for not really ever *finishing* projects around the house before I start a next), I was back to traveling for work, and the cat sitter, Kimber, was coming far more than I wished Killer needed to be alone other than for those twice-a-day visits.

I had met Kimber through an app, and she is probably one of the first people that I really got to know other than my neighbors since I had moved to Florida. I think she was partial to watching dogs (I do understand that in many ways they are more engaging), but she accepted my request to watch Killer often without hesitation. We met, set up all the necessary agreements and such, and Kimber watched Killer for the better part of two years for me before my second-youngest niece, Melayna, moved in to complete her studies online in a new, warmer, and mom-free environment.

There were stretches when Killer needed four or five days or even a whole week of watching, and it often broke my heart to think of her being in bed alone for so long. She did seem to adjust well, or at least as judged by how she greeted me just the same—running toward the door when she heard my keys jangle—no matter how long I had been away. As it turns out, I suppose I encouraged that by always bringing her a new selection of treats from wherever I had been, and especially if there was a little local pet store in the area. But even so, I didn't like her to be by herself so much, even when I knew that Kimber stayed a lot longer than her fifteen-minute commitment twice a day (and her son often joined or came by separately, too).

Knowing that travel was going to pick up as the school year started to near its end—summer professional development was my high season—I decided to get Killer a companion for the time when the sitter was not at the house. Killer had grown up around dogs (to her displeasure as I mentioned) and other cats (to less displeasure, but still), so I was sure that she would welcome a new cat into the mix with whom she could play while I was gone. Killer perhaps was not as sure I found out.

~

When I first went to see Nightmare, who was too young to adopt at that visit, I fell in love with her right away (and I kind of think she did with me, too). She is all black except for a small shield of white on her chest, which only shows when she stands at attention. She let me hold her close but was not a fan of a little kiss on the forehead—I suppose not a lot of kittens are when our exaggerated kiss lips are coming toward their faces! She sniffed to check me out and then rested her head quietly to look over my shoulder. That's when I felt *him.*

Turns out that Nightmare has a little very protective brother. Although today he is called Silverado, at the moment his claws and my lower legs met, I had another name going through my head (although I softened it by prefixing it with *"little")*. His attacks were very haphazard—as many strikes of his tiny but sharp claws landed in mid-air as on my legs and feet, and at least twice my shoestrings got the better of him and he had to detangle and regroup before returning to the frontline. As it was, however, Killer would now have two companions: an almost-all-black sister and a white tabby brother.

Once home, I kept the little ones separated in my room for several days, exchanging their blankets and beds for Killer's blankets and beds so they would learn about each other through scent. They visited a lot at the crack at the bottom of the door to my room, which gave them some time to adjust, but they did not meet face-to-face until the end of that "getting to smell you" week. I don't think Killer minded sleeping in the guest bedroom during that time—I put my blanket and pillows there in the hopes that she would think I was coming any minute, but I did stay with the little ones because I didn't know what they would do alone all night.

It turns out, they do a lot. Before the week was out, they had learned how to scale the mattress to get on the bed, and they scaled the curtains just as easily (adding curtains to the shopping list). They showed me that shoestrings were far more exciting than any toy I can order—although my feet under the sheet were a very close second (I draped a comforter over the bottom edge for safety). And, if you are in the market for night table lamps, I can tell you for sure where to order some glass ones that do not break when they fall on the floor. I enjoyed those first few nights, anyway, because I had not had kittens before. I especially liked that they snuggled with one another as brother and sister, and they do this even today.

~

Killer and the kittens finally met on a Saturday morning right before breakfast. A little tentative review from across the room, a hesitant return to the bedroom for Silverado before he came back out, and a slightly disapproving flick of the tail by Killer that she and I needed to rid the house of these characters provides a complete description of this introduction. But the din of breakfast plates and cans popping open distracted them long enough to come together, and after a bit of sniffing, they seemed to suggest they were going to get along just fine.

Killer shares her water fountain and politely waits when one of them uses it just because she is headed toward it. She finds another scratcher snuggler bed when a kitten takes her favorite one by the lanai doors, and she gently moves aside during a brushing so that one of them can come closer and share the brush. Overall, Killer is mostly accommodating to them, and they respond by quietly deferring to her guidance.

However, it is clear sometimes that she is frustrated, too—but she marches off to her safe spots instead of choosing to fight them! I appreciate that. She doesn't like them using her litter box, so I had to get her a new one. She expresses dismay as much as a cat can when they think they are part of the bedtime plan: a little noise and a dramatic exit follow anytime one of the little ones begins to make biscuits on the blanket as a sign of settling-in for the night– but soon Killer is back in her spot. And when Nightmare finishes her own meal (she was the runt and is very food-oriented) and assumes that Killer simply eats slowly in order to share, Killer sets the record straight firmly but without incident.

~

By the time the kittens grew to adults, they had never really become Killer's friends. I think now that she probably never wanted a companion–I wanted her to have one. But she does get at least part of what I wanted because they do run after each other a little for fun, sometimes nap in the same room, and otherwise coexist while never exactly showing that they are best friends to each other as I thought they might. But they do, however, acknowledge one another's needs and respect that each is a valuable part of the family.

~

Killer welcomed the kittens into our home and showed patience and tolerance as we all learned to navigate new relationships and lifestyles. I considered how often I had offered the same to others as easily as she.

~

Patience is not my virtue, which is the only modification of or cliché itself I intend to use in this story. I think I learned it from my dad. While my brother will go to the bathroom before the check comes at a restaurant, my dad just begins to tap his wallet on the table—seemingly the three- or four-minute wait is too much for him! He's always been impatient about things like that, and I certainly see a lot of him in my patience limits.

The Oxford dictionary offers the following definition for *patience*:

"[T]he capacity to accept or tolerate delay, trouble, or suffering without getting angry or upset."

I have been known to scream at red lights (that probably lasted no more than sixty seconds), sigh out loud when the cashier at a grocery store bags slowly, or when someone at work starts a presentation with an icebreaker. As I think about it, not even one of those things changes because I grow impatient. Instead, I grow annoyed, but it is only shared by me (or sometimes, the unfortunate passenger). I'll reread the mindfulness chapter if it happens again!

Killer, on the other hand, is very good at being patient at a delay. I admire that about her. (Now, you should note that this does not apply as much to breakfast–but that's probably her only bother.) Like I said, she will easily defer to the kittens at the water fountain, when the feather is being flown around the bedroom, or when the automatic laser light begins to track running paths for them around the floor (even though that's her favorite toy).

Over the past two years especially, I have made more of an effort to show patience with people and things that I previously let bother me. Part of that is because I take more time to put small disturbances in perspective–I better position things that annoy me into the bigger picture of what's really important and what isn't. Alone, I recognize the value of peace for myself and think about all the blessings I have before I let something get to me. When interacting with others, I now better consider what their story might be: what's happening in their lives, what news did they get today, how will their interaction with me be remembered?

~

I clearly saw patience from Killer as she managed living with the kittens– very little irritability when they jumped on her and calmness when they ran around on the floor while she was napping. I wondered, though, was it more than just a simple patience? I mean, they were so different than her, and they had come into her home without her invitation! Yes; I did see more than just patience–I also saw a tolerance that she showed us all. Along with patience, I suppose, this tolerance is what I have seen become absent in social discourse. There appears to be so little if we watch the news now (so I no longer do), but I am reassured because I don't see it in my everyday interactions with others here and in my travels.

The Oxford dictionary gives the following definition for *tolerance*:

"[T]he ability or willingness to tolerate something, in particular the existence of opinions or behavior that one does not necessarily agree with."

The tolerance that I see Killer offer the kittens is not premised on them being like her, and she does not take offense to their being paired while she is a single cat without siblings. There are no requirements they show proof of their origin to join us, and she by no means expects them to have lesser than she as she shares her beds, scratchers, toys, and treats. And there is no sign that she is bothered because they meow with a slightly different rhythm. I thought about that tolerance when I was with my niece in New York City a while back.

I've more than once heard someone say, "They should learn our language." I hate hearing that, because right at that moment "they" just don't know it! It's tolerance to show compassion and empathy to provide a little help if you can or at least to try to find out how you can support someone in immediate need. My second-oldest niece knows just *un poco* Spanish, but she stopped to try to understand a woman who was trying to buy a ticket on the New

Jersey Transit system a few weeks ago—a woman who others had ignored. Instead of dismissing her with a shoulder shrug, Domonique listened carefully and encouraged her to repeat what she needed. I'm very proud of her for that.

And, in some ways, that is exactly the tolerance that Killer shows for the kittens. She isn't exactly sure what they are saying and she has little knowledge of their background. Nonetheless, they are part of the family and she is going to treat them as such.

~

Although Killer sees a lot of what the kittens do as disruptive, perhaps—I mean, they do try to bite her tail—with patience and tolerance she accepts as they learn how to become cats in our home.

6

Lesson Four: Expectations & Needs

As I mentioned, I mostly travel to do my work, so when I am home there is no urgency to get up as early as I might if I was on the road. I often sleep until shortly after 6:30 in the morning, or even sometimes go to bed later the evening before and laze in bed until 8:00—long after the sun has already arrived in the old dining room where Killer would soon be. But, before she arrives there, several tasks in preparation for the big show of the morning—breakfast—need completion.

Like all cats (and, to some degree, humans), Killer enjoys the rhythm of any day to be much like the rhythm of every day. She is keen to get up at about the same time each morning and slowly check out things as she makes her way back to the bedroom to be sure I know it is time to serve her the morning meal, which is usually a liver or chicken or whatever, as she prefers the seafood pâté in the evening.

~

I had earlier gotten Killer a cat tree with various shelves, hammocks, and scratching posts, but she had grown a little big to make the jumps needed to scale it. (The vet said this was fine, as she was not overweight *enough* to cause concern.) So, I dismantled the upper sections, and it became a couple of platforms and a ladder onto the longer kitchen counter for her where the water fountain was located (and her respite area from the little ones). And anyway, I thought a little exercise might be forced by not keeping things on the floor. She also has started to take her meals there, which I suppose is because she wants to ensure the little ones see her as superior. This cat tree figures big in her daily routine. Let me share with you her unwavering schedule of morning activity.

7:15 am: Arrival at her litter box to…um…prepare room for today's treats and meals. This was an unusually elaborate affair. Once finished, she scratches the upper interior sides of the litter box as if she is an artist painting a fresco—gentle, wide scratches back-and-forth as if she is wielding a paintbrush—but accomplishing nothing in terms of concealing the main purpose of her visit. This can go on for as long as ten minutes, as she repositions, finds a new corner that she had missed, or just needs to make that final adjustment to her mind's eye painting. Now, if she is discovered in this phase, she will immediately jump out and run, so she certainly wants this to be a private moment. I can relate (but with three cats I don't know how that feels anymore).

7:30 am: As you might expect, the mural work takes a lot out of her, so next she hops up on the counter to get her first drink of the day. Killer is an avid drinker. While I had heard that cats didn't need as much water as dogs, no one has told her that. She can be found as many as fifteen or more times at the water fountain each day, and after a few sips she'll lie loafing and looking around at the floors for any intruders for a few minutes. At her first morning stop, she'll sit down, glance around the room for a while, take a few sips, survey the dining room, and repeat that a few times before hopping down—it seems to be kind of like a "morning coffee" moment for her.

7:40 am: This is appetizer time for her. Below the cat tree, a bowl of kibble (Iams Indoor for Healthy Weight—but don't tell her it's a diet version!). She pauses to sniff the bowlful of food that is always the same; I guess the sniff is simply confirmatory, and it reassures her that it's fine to take a few nibbles to get her day started. She purrs her way through maybe twenty or thirty small pieces before, it seems, she remembers that it's getting closer to eight. And that's a big deal for her.

A quick succession of checks and pauses follows before arriving back to my room: scratch on the curved scratcher by the living room couch (*7:47 am*), garden survey at the window (*7:50 am*), review of boxes that came in yesterday from Amazon that are awaiting unpacking or breaking down (*7:52 am*, if needed), checking to see if anyone is in the ensuite bathroom (*7:54 am*), walk-in closet overview as she passes by

(*7:56 am*), and a long, sit-down pause before moving into my bedroom (*7:58 am-7:59 am*).

8:00 am: Because she expects breakfast at the same time every morning, Killer starts by scratching the walls, and she believes that removing paint is okay. If that is not enough, then she starts meowing—not a sweet, subtle meowing that gently wakes you up but a horrifying howling-type meowing, as if a paw got caught in a rotating tool in the garage. Finally, although rarely do I need this third-level approach, she can be found both of those on the bed in my face, with my face taking the place of the wall. Ouch. (I should note that she acknowledges I am more sensitive than a wall, and she adjusts for that in her intensity.)

Killer takes her breakfast, as I mentioned, on the counter near her cat tree. She sits patiently while I open the can, scoop it out onto her plate, and break it apart because I think that little bites are more appealing to her than a big chunk. She eats far more daintily than she behaves when she is placing her order in the bedroom. In fact, she delights in eating, and she eats very slowly, moving around the plate when a particularly juicy piece of the breakfast on the far edge catches her eye. She might circle around the plate five or six times before the meal is over.

Killer is a gravy lover. She likes to start with the liquid that separates from the pâté as it creates a moat around the mushy bits, and she savors each lick of the plate before taking the next. Often, I will get her cans of food that are more broth, gravy, or stew-like, which she enjoys very much—but she likes pâté so much that she won't eat enough of the shreds, pieces, or chunks found in those to make a meal. But she will always visit the little ones' plates in case they left some liquid behind.

8:20ish am-late afternoon: At the end of breakfast, Killer grooms on my desk in the old dining room, and then she naps a little bit before I grab the brush when she lets me know she'd like a little brushing. She enjoys being brushed quite a lot. I am grateful for that because, as a Russian Blue, she has a full body of fur that at times almost allows you to track her movements around the house as small puffs of fur fall behind her at different times of the year. Again, she hops up onto the cat tree, takes her position on the counter, and she revels in brushing for as long as I give her the time to do it. She gets brushed when she asks—I'll talk more about that soon—and this is a great time for us to bond a bit without the other two in the way (although if they hear it going on long enough, the little ones might come to take a peek or get a little bit, themselves).

Killer takes to her nap routines once I start working at the computer when I need to. She prefers to lie in a bed near me to start the day, and she has been doing this since she first came into my life. I really enjoy that because for a long time she and I were the only two in the house, and it brings great comfort to know that she will be there when I take a break. She has grown to expect a tussle with the feather toy or a scratch behind her ears from time-to-time throughout the day.

5:00 pm: Dinner time comes with less fanfare than breakfast, and I suppose that is because I am already up and aware that it's 5:00 pm. Of course, Killer is a timepiece of her own, and she'll remind me more gently if I don't notice. Same deal as breakfast (although it's always seafood at dinner), and she purrs just the same while watching her meal being made.

5:20ish pm-bedtime: The rest of a typical evening is spent on the lanai while I read a book or take a swim, or sometimes I will go kayak for a bit and she'll just watch the butterflies, lizards, and birds in the back garden through the lanai screen while she awaits my return. Often, she has some evening front-yard time to enjoy the cooler air that takes over when the sun has passed to the backyard. Later, she knows that the lights off in the living room mean we head to the bedroom, where she takes her spot, makes some biscuits, and prepares to get a good night's rest.

What I think keeps Killer so happy and content is that she knows what to expect and knows that there's another person on whom she can count. And I'm happy that she lets me know what she needs, whether that's a good meal or some time to play and be a cat. Of course, she also lets me know when she needs to be alone and take some time for herself–I've yet to figure out how she knows the same for me!

~

Although our human relationships are different in so many ways, they are still at their foundation built on expectations and needs. Why do we seem to be afraid to make these known?

~

Shortly before moving to Florida, I had started into a relationship that lasted a couple of years, including just a short stretch after I moved. I had met him in Alexandria, and we started bike riding and hiking, going out to restaurants and music venues, and spending time taking his dog for a walk. He was very much oriented toward his family, which was a bit unfamiliar to me—I did not get to see mine as much as I wanted, and often when I did it never quite went as well as my mind had pictured. He and I had frequent game nights with his family, celebrated birthdays with some fanfare, and spent a lot of time just hanging out watching movies with them, going to Dave & Buster's, or enjoying the pool once the hot Washington summer settled in.

I'm pretty sure I spent more time with his family in the time we dated than with much of my own totaled over the last twenty years. I enjoyed his family very much—I think about mine now in the context of my experience with them and Killer.

~

We had been close enough as a family growing up. I mean, trips to the mall on Fridays (there was an arcade at Southwyck Mall, and my brother and I each got a few dollars to play), and we used to go up to the Renaissance Center's Westin hotel in Detroit a few times each summer so we could go to the international festivals in Hart Plaza. It was exciting to stay on such a high floor in a hotel, and I recall having fun walking around Detroit's downtown, eating interesting new foods, and hearing live music.

We would take family trips, of course, to see other family, as well. Usually at Thanksgiving or Christmas we would travel to Mansfield and visit with my mom's side of the family—we saw my dad's side more often because they lived in Toledo, which is where I grew up. Sometimes we would go to his mom's lake house near the western edge of Ohio, and me and my brother would get to stay a few nights there.

But soon after we had all moved out of the house (my parents had separated when I was in early high school), we didn't see each other as much. Even when we all lived in the same city—I didn't leave for Washington, DC until 2001—we didn't seem to make it much of a priority to see one another. We talked on the phone sometimes, and certainly we did take time for quick visits now and then, but we lost somewhere speaking the *expectations* and *needs* of the relationships we could have with each other—really, that we wanted with each other—and spoke less and less about anything over time. I can see that without articulating wishes and hopes, there isn't a force behind the relationships to keep them strong.

~

Killer loves one more thing about as equal as treats. I mentioned that as a Russian Blue, she has a lot of hair. I mean a lot. When she first moved in, she got a lot of hairballs, and I found them around the house—usually on a rug instead of the easy-to-clean wood floor. (I've noticed this is a thing with cats.) They were quite large hairballs, and they were mixed with whatever liquid in their bodies that also occupies the place where hairballs await their formal presentation onto the rug. Just nasty.

It looked like it was very difficult to produce one of these hairballs, so I decided to start brushing her more during those first weeks together. Like I said, she could lie on the counter all day flipping from side-to-side to get those hairs off! I start along the center of her back, which sets her into a frenzy of rolling around to feel the bristles over her whole body (except the belly). Once the initial high is over, she gently rolls left-to-right and back again until I stop when I don't see much hair left on the brush–usually it's about fifteen minutes of brushing.

Now, Killer lets me know when she wants a good brushing. She meows at the brush setting on the counter and nudges the brush when I come over to uncover the cause of her current fuss. She knows something that I am finally learning: it's important to just tell people what you need.

~

In the last few years, my siblings and I have become more vocal about what we want our relationships to look like. Now, my sister has spent almost whole summers with me, and my brother has come down to spend time–but he's very antsy, so he needs a project to do while away or he simply won't leave home. And I've been back to visit them a lot more since Killer showed me how to just be more open about needs and expectations.

The toughest relationship in the family to get back has been the one with my mom. It's not just what I want from her, it's what I want to be able to give her, too, of course. Living in Florida, there are a lot of older folks her age (although it's changing fast as younger people and families move here). I see sons my age with their moms at the Twisted Fork listening to rock music bands on Friday nights, I see them out for dinner at late into the evenings, and I see them shopping at University Town Center just to spend some time together. I would enjoy doing those things with her.

I had an expectation that she would have come to my Ph.D. commencement ten years ago, which she did not. I resented her a bit for that, but there's a whole chapter later about being more ready to offer forgiveness—so I know now how wasteful that emotion was. Instead, I should have told her how much I wanted her to be there, and what need it satisfied for both of us. I've learned that now, and I will continue to find ways to engage with her to build the relationship that meets our needs and expectations to help us both find pleasure in what it brings.

~

The couple-yearslong romantic relationship that was so exciting and reminded me of how much I missed family interactions ended cordially shortly after I moved to Florida. Like in so many other parts of my life, I had then yet to learn to define expectations, speak needs, and outline boundaries—and he was as poor at it as me. We had spent a lot of time thinking the other was expected to know what's on the other's mind—and that's not fair to either person. Killer makes her expectations clear, and I acknowledge her needs because of that. I wonder how that relationship would have worked out had I learned doing that better just a little bit earlier.

What I did get out of the relationship beyond reflecting on how I could do better with needs and expectations at work, with family, and in a new relationship was a cat. See, Killer was his sister's before she was mine. She had to rehome Killer when she moved, and I had long before that decided that Killer was pretty remarkable—and her name made me believe she was a bit of a wild girl. So, of course I took her in when she needed a place to be.

~

Even today, she is not a wild girl, but I do know why we get along so well: we're both teachers.

7

Lesson Five: Well-Being

I first heard the terrifying, new sound shortly after I went to bed one night after we had been in the house for about two years. Was it an injured bird outside? Or was it fighting cats out by the canal—it sounded a lot like what you might here in that case, too. Or maybe it's the sound of some other animal that I was still unfamiliar with—I surely had not seen all the wildlife this quickly growing area was pushing in all directions. I got up quickly and looked around the living room and dining room because it sounded like it could just as easily have been coming from there as beyond the lanai. I flipped on the lights (well, I asked Siri to turn them on...it was 2023).

I didn't see much of note: Silverado on the chair and Killer sitting by the cat tree just looking at me as if I was weird for being up in the middle of the night—unaware that I might have said the same of her. Nightmare was coming from my room, so I knew she was not the source of this sound. Over the next several nights (and even until today) this noise continued, and I finally isolated it to being a vocalization that Killer was performing during a little almost-ritual she has developed.

I had bought some little catnip-laced toy mice for the little ones for their birthday on April 21st, and it seems that Killer adopted the orange-eared, orange-tailed ones as her own. No others—just the two with orange. At night, after everyone goes to sleep, she gathers her little charges near a cat scratcher by the dining room and puts them to bed, but she has to make this noise for whatever reason—and it is loud and continues for about ten minutes or so. There she is, wailing away while placing the little cotton ovals with eyes and tails on their cardboard bed. Why? To announce they are asleep? To soothe them to sleep? (Not that sound!) Maybe it's just for her. At any rate, once she settled those little mice into their sleep, she was unbothered for the rest of the night and slept as usual until morning.

She carries these two little tattered mice around with her throughout the day. They can be found sleeping between her front paws, and it is not unusual to find one concealed in the sheets and blankets on your bed. They have even been known to get a washing machine bath, which does not deter her from knowing these two are hers even with a hint of Tide on them. It's fun to watch her look for them, carry them around, and apparently care for them as she goes about her day.

In some way those little mice bring her comfort or safety. She really will not go to sleep until she knows they are safe in their bed—I've seen her run around the house, zip under beds, hop onto shelving, and even unload entire laundry baskets to find these little guys. I think it's nice that she has them.

(We could not find them at one time because they had become mingled in with some bedsheets that were being washed—and that sat later in a basket waiting to be folded. So, we got another set. Do not try to trick a cat.)

~

I have a lot of shoes. A lot of people wonder why I have so many shoes. My dad visited a while back and counted them. I would rather not say how many he counted. (Although some are slides or sandals or used only for outdoor work, which I would argue don't count in the total.) He thought out loud that maybe he's never owned that many in his whole lifetime. But what he also doesn't own is a cat.

See, it turns out that when you buy a new pair of shoes, you are also getting a cat toy: a box. And it's not even just a toy—it can be a bed, too! So, I'm not really overbuying shoes, I am simply buying toys and beds for the cats; the toys and beds just happen to come with shoes in them. And Killer loves it.

As you read, Killer has a little belly she carries around, but, again, it's not like she is unhealthy overweight, which my vet confirms. She's just an older cat that enjoys food, treats, napping, and exercise (like walking to get treats or finding a place to nap). She also likes new boxes. In fact, it is this belly that requires she gets new boxes.

I am a size nine-and-a-half in tennis shoes. However, Killer is a size eleven in tennis shoe boxes—and therein lies the reason that I have to replace these boxes more frequently than one might think I should need to. She is partial to Nike.

Killer runs toward the orange box when I place it on the floor. I always leave the tissue paper in it because she also likes the sound of crumpling paper. She gives it a few sniffs, rubs ears and cheeks along its corners, and gives a few tentative prodding strokes to the interior before she finally fully steps in. Once in, she turns a few times and then nestles in with her head held high that she claimed it before any other cat even knew it was available. Soon, her chin is resting on the attached lid as she falls asleep. A few repositionings later, and I think she has given the box the form it needs to keep her happy.

After some time—maybe a few weeks or even fewer if the box is out on the lanai in the humid Florida summer—you see the first corner tearing. And you have already seen the bulging front side of the box developing for some time. Killer doesn't take exception to the distorted shape the box has taken, but I know that it is nearing the end of its useful life, as it will just be a few more full turns before the corners yield to a burden for which a shoe box was not built.

It happens rather abruptly that a box's corners decide they have had enough. It is, of course, always when she is in it that this happens, and she lurches forward (or backward, depending on her orientation at that moment) as the box spills its pudgy contents onto the floor. Surprised but unharmed, she inspects the box, acknowledges its uninhabitable condition, and moves on. No matter, I guess, she has enjoyed the box more than I would have ever thought a cat might.

And I head to Footlocker.

~

Killer doesn't need much. She has several little beds around the house, yet she chooses the scratchers for rest instead. And, although the whole length of the couch could be hers, there are other places to which she would rather lay claim as safe and comforting.

Maybe it was during an interval between boxes that Killer discovered how much she liked lying on the chair on the lanai. It rocked, so while it was always a graceful approach as cats are disposed to display, the landing was less than elegant. She tentatively places a paw on the cushion and gives it a little push test, and then slowly brings the other one to meet it. Once the chair settles its initial slight back-and-forth, she springs onto the chair and wobbles for a few seconds (the wobble is getting a little longer with each treat–Newton's third law is real), carefully firming herself with four paws and all claws pressed into the cushion while she stares around as if she this was her first experience. Once she is comfortably assured that the motion is over, she makes her biscuits, completes a few turns, and settles into a curl.

She likes the Murphy bed in the guest bedroom, too. Bypassing several choices along the way, she sits in front of the vertical wood panels of the raised bed and meows softly. She turns her head from time-to-time to see if I have yet to drop what I am doing to tend to her immediate need! Whether it's the smooth outer texture of the feather-filled, puffy comforter that makes her find the end of that bed so welcoming or just the uniqueness of it being made available just for her, she easily finds her comfortable spot and loafs or curls up there until it's time to move on.

In all these things, Killer finds a safe place or a comfort that reassures her life is good. What was there yesterday is still here today, and you can see she loves that.

~

Comfort, security, and well-being. All of these remind Killer that she is home and safe. I thought a bit about how I bring the same to others and myself.

~

Comfort, security, and well-being are related but different concepts. Killer displays all of them. The comfort that her Nike boxes bring her. The security of knowing that her little mice are tucked in and accounted for. Her well-being, then, is what comfort and security bring to her. She finds a lot of ways to find these on her own, but I find ways, too, that I believe will bring them to her: trying different foods until I find the one she likes the best or giving her access to different places to be (like out front, the lanai, or the guest bedroom). Together, we seek out and act on those opportunities that build trust, relax one another, and provide an environment that enhances stability rather than creates stress, anxiety, and fear.

~

Comfort is one of those words that takes on so many meanings in everyday life. It is often thought of as freedom from pain and suffering, as in comforting someone who is in mourning or recovering from an illness or injury. It's also reassurance, such as when we comfort a loved one who has lost a job or something else important to them that things will get better. And we even use it as an adjective to describe food types! Any number of hot meals that always include a lot of fat, butter, and calories that we use when we need to feel better about something more mundane like having a bad day are our comfort foods.

Of course I do some of that type of comforting with Killer, as we all do with folks (and pets), like when I close the bedroom door during a storm and turn the fan on high so that it makes enough noise to drown out the thunder. Or when there is a lot of commotion because the kittens have the zoomies and I give Killer a silvervine stick in the guest bedroom on the Murphy bed. Those are what I think of as *responses of comfort*—ways we react to a friend, a loved one, or even ourselves to help us and them to feel better or cope with situations. But Killer showed me that comfort was not just a response to offer—indeed, when unfailing, comfort itself leads to its own responses. And maybe thinking of it like this more often helped me to get through some uncertain times when we first moved together.

Creating comfort in someone's life is an ongoing promise. For me, it is Killer's unyielding commitment to landing next to me in bed at night (at least until she got older and decided to sleep with Melayna). In that sense, comfort is kind of like creating a reliance upon which someone can count. For Killer, it is knowing that when she runs to the door when I get home after being gone for a day or two there is a treat in the bag I bring in from the car. In that sense, comfort is like an affirmation—a confidence that someone is thinking of you even when separated. And for both of us, it is knowing that mornings start with coffee on the lanai and evening ends with a book on the couch. In that sense, comfort is the tradition or habit that provides dependability and evenness to a relationship.

And, so, I think that the comfort I learn from Killer is only sometimes the response to something–thinking more broadly, in most cases it creates the responses: happiness, certainty, and trust among them.

~

Killer is not pleased when the trash truck goes by. Like I mentioned, not many cars go down the street because there are only three houses on the circle, which means that very little action occurs. The dogs barking or the whirring of a golf cart are often the only things we'll hear in a day. But on Fridays when Killer is out in the front yard, her ears stiffen, and she looks around as the rumbles of the truck get closer while it marches toward the can at the edge of the driveway.

As it turns the corner off the main road onto the circle, Killer gets up from the driveway and makes her way closer to me and the front door. She trots just a little bit faster when the driver gives it some gas after the slower-speed turn he had to make requires him to get some speed to get going again—she turns her head rapidly between forward-looking and backward-looking as she confirms both her path to the front door and keeps an eye in the direction from which the sound is coming. Ignoring all the lizards that on another day would have become her playthings must be hard for her! Once she sees the truck, her eyes grow huge, she meows that she is a bit scared (or at least alarmed), and I open the front door so she can go in. Phew...that was close, I suspect she thinks.

This story of her weekly interaction with the trash truck reminds me that she finds security in our home. For her, all the commotion, unknown, and danger is beyond the spaces where she feels safe and cared for. She can find a corner, a bed, or a counter to lie on and know that she is shielded from the real or imagined threats elsewhere.

Killer confirmed for me that it is important to ensure that a home is made to feel as the safest place available for important people in our lives—especially when that is a partner or loved one. See, there is no place else for Killer to feel safe, and it's so clear now that there isn't either for me or anyone I choose to bring into my life. That means that I have to work harder to prevent anger toward, arguments between, and irritation with people from taking that security away at home. And it might not be bad to practice that better anywhere I happen to be.

~

And that leads us to well-being. There are so many elements of well-being for us to think about: physical and emotional well-being, social well-being, and even work well-being. I want to share a story that I think illustrates how having a sense of purpose and connection creates well-being.

Killer may sense that I have emotional responses to having her around. I won't belabor the ways in which she provokes those, as you've read so much about it already; but it's true. It certainly involves the enjoyment of having someone around the house, the responsibility of being able to take care of her, and the warm-heartedness that feeling important (even to a cat) brings me. She is a source of well-being in her own right.

~

My mom got her first cat this year. Well, it's really a kitten. Her doctor said that it might help her because she's alone more now that the great-grandkids have gotten older and spend more time with their friends and less time at her house. I encouraged her to follow-through without a doubt! She named him Pixel, and he's quite the little wild boy. No worry, she's learning how to manage with him, although she's had lots of questions!

I sent her a big welcome package for Pixel because getting to the store is a lot for her, and, too, the cost is more of a burden on her than me now that she has long been retired. Besides, it was a lot of fun for me to pick out kitten stuff again, which I have not had to do in awhile. Pixel got, of course, all the essentials like food, cute bowls, feather toys, litter, and a litter box. I also made sure he had a few scratching pads, and he got his first cat tree (although it's right-sized for him—he's only two-and-a-half pounds and can't really jump much yet).

She is so much more alive with Pixel! He keeps her on her toes because she has to interact with him constantly given that he's a curious brand-new kitten. She seems to not have the same melancholy tone in her voice when we talk on the phone, and she's engaging with neighbors as they come to visit her new "son." She and I even went shopping together for the first time in years to find things for Pixel when I visited in the spring, and we had breakfast at Bob Evans–it might have been ten years since I've been out like that with her! I think that for her Pixel has brought some purpose, fulfilled some needs, and created a sharing with others that was absent before. And those things have improved her well-being in multiple ways. I am happy to see that.

In a sense, Pixel joining the family with her has improved my well-being, too. Although it's just been a few months, she and I talk so much more (with a ton of laughing), we text pictures of the cats to each other to share in his first things, and we get to talk about a lot of other stuff because this silly cat has gotten us on the phone together. And to Bob Evans.

8

Lesson Six: Forgiveness

W e've been a few years in the house in Florida now, and you have read quite a lot about bits and pieces of our lives together. For a few years now Killer has just continued living her best life, and I enjoy that I've had the chance to share that with her.

But I was never a cat guy. I had always been a dog guy. Killer was my first cat, and I was unsure how I was going to adapt from an animal that unquestionably shows you how much he is excited to see you, who needs walks every day, and who wags his tail at just the sound of your car pulling in the driveway to an animal that *might* show you how excited she is to see you, that never needs walks, and that uses its tail in so many ways it is really hard to know what she is telling you!

~

Petey was a little Jack Russell (dad) and West Highland Terrier (mom) mix that I rewarded myself with when I finished my doctoral program at George Mason University in 2014. I had always wanted a dog as an adult, but I had not really considered it while I was teaching because I knew that I would be gone all day, and I didn't really like the idea of that. But I switched jobs shortly after graduating, and it meant more time at home unless I was traveling, so I figured it was a good time to bring a dog home.

I found Petey at the Alexandria Animal Welfare League facility, and I remember the day like it was yesterday. I was headed home, and instead of going straight on Van Dorn Avenue, I decided to make the right turn onto Eisenhower and head over to the animal shelter—I'm still not sure why I thought that day was the right one. They welcomed me at the door and took me back to see all the dogs available for adoption–there were so many! People have so many reasons that they become unable to care for their pets, and I understand that folks had made difficult decisions in most cases to take them there.

A lot of dogs were barking, and many of them were jumping up and down on their cages to attract attention. I convinced myself that they were doing it to audition and not because they simply wanted a petting, a treat, or a touch–something the volunteers tried to spread around but were often too overwhelmed to do consistently. However, one of the dogs was not barking. He just sat in the back of his cage waiting for dinner. And that was Petey. He caught my eye because of that, and then I noticed how small he was–less than 20 pounds and perfectly able to sit on a lap. Living in a two-story condominium in West Alexandria it made sense to get a small dog. So, I spent some time with him in the adoption room, and he and I decided this was a fit. I took Petey home a few days later.

Petey settled-in just fine, and on the first night he knew that the bed was where he slept– at our feet, so as to not be too much of an intrusion. Petey had just turned nine, so he already knew what life was like with humans. We liked that about him because it meant there was no real learning curve for him in adapting to his new home and not a lot for us to need to train.

But it wasn't his home for long. We really thought that he needed more space to be a dog, so we sold the condo the following year and moved into a single-family home with a large backyard with trees to lie under and squirrels for him to chase (he never actually caught one). Although he enjoyed the new back yard, he was more often found inside with one of us playing with a chew toy or just lying alongside on the couch or the floor. He seemed to want to remind us how much he appreciated that we picked him.

Over the next few years, Petey grew tired a little more quickly, he had more trouble making it outdoors when he needed to go, and he slept a lot more than he used to. He didn't play as much, and he seemed a lot less interested in long walks in favor of just a quick jot to the end of the street. We accommodated him, of course, in various ways, and he still made sure to show us the signs that dogs use to message that they are happy.

But, in the February just before the Covid-19 pandemic exploded, Petey showed signs of being in distress. We took him to the hospital, and they were confident that it was fluids and some rest he needed. After three days of trying to get better, we knew that his little body just wasn't going to let him live the life he deserved and that we promised to him. He shared in five years of joy, and he never held it against the humans that he had to spend over a year—in two stints, even!—in a shelter waiting for someone to give him a home. Petey dived in with confidence on the first day in his new home and never looked back. Then, on his last day, we affirmed our commitment to him that he would not be allowed to suffer.

~

Killer is now almost five years older than when I first met her, and she is slowing down a bit. She doesn't show any signs of illness or anything, she's just a bit slower than before as far as I can tell. She plays and eats just the same, but she is having a few accidents; she tends to really like the couch for that. Ugh.

Killer has been known in the past to do this, so at first I just suspected the little ones are getting on her nerves, or maybe they are using her litter box (I earlier told you that she requires an exclusive litter box). Now, to me those are silly reasons, and it annoys me that she thinks it is fine. Even a small dribble took almost a half hour to clean, and it was even longer if I didn't notice it until later. I'll admit that I yell and scream a bit out of frustration when I discover a new puddle but never at her directly. Instead, I kind of just yell at the world that this is ridiculous and that there is no need to not use the box like she has for fourteen years! Well, as much as her peeing on the couch and rugs bothers me, the yelling scares her, and she goes under my bed, which makes me promise to both of us that I will never yell in frustration again. But I do.

Once cleaned up, Killer comes out to find me and rub along my leg as if to say she is sorry, and I stroke her or scratch behind her ears to tell her the same. Then, I give her a few treats, which I guess I think comforts her to know I am not mad at her. Of course, I kind of am, but I know that to be a waste because she isn't doing it to be bad, she is doing it because something is bothering her—but that is small comfort when I have to find a way to keep my furniture from being ruined. At any rate, I do my best to reassure her that everything is okay.

Moving forward a few weeks, the couch is covered in plastic, and she has a new litter box that is seeming to do the trick. It is also moved into my niece Melayna's room (she has become a real friend to Killer—equal to the friend that Killer has become to her).

While I am not sure the problem is solved, I know that Killer forgives me for the yelling. I think, too, that Petey forgave his first humans for putting him in a shelter—they surely had a reason.

~

These little pets seem to forgive our mistakes pretty easily. Maybe they know that forgiving unburdens the heart and makes it available for so much.

~

I've forgiven easily in the past. My dad said to me a few years ago that he wished for forgiveness for the chaos and missed experiences because he and my mom divorced. He even asked if I had forgiven him. I missed things that other kids had with their dads, sure. But I graduated, went on to college, and later developed a relationship with him that I consider the most important and valuable in my life.

That example of forgiveness is how psychologists talk about the three kinds: exoneration, forbearance, and release. Each requires a certain type of precedent harm— intentional or not. Exoneration results when forgiveness is afforded due to unintentional harm—think something like inviting all your friends to dinner but forgetting one member of the group. He will forgive you by simply wiping the slate clean even though he was hurt by the forgotten invitation. Forbearance is that forgiveness we offer when we decide it's time to no longer be upset even if the offender hasn't taken full responsibility. This is kind of like moving forward but needing to learn to trust the other again. Finally, the last is the most liberating in many ways: release. This occurs when *we* decide to just let it go. Whatever it was might have been hurtful, but we need to release ourselves from it even if the other person has not offered any kind of apology—when we do this it is most often someone that is no longer a part of one's life, and we're just carrying the burden alone, anyway.

Of course, forgiveness is among the most valuable acts in our relationships; however, although I am a social scientist, psychology is not my game. So, let me steer away from it in this light before I go too far! But the reason I want to move on is because I don't want to talk about the psychology of forgiveness, I want to talk about what Killer elevated and opened my eyes to. See, there are two more facets of forgiveness she's helped me to think about: to simply be more forgiving and forgiving myself. Killer helped me to focus on these, and I think it's important because maybe they are the two more salient in our everyday lives.

~

On evenings when work meetings run a little over or I go to the gym later than planned, I am late with Killer's dinner; you might already understand how this is very bothersome to her. She meows and fusses, and once she notices I am finished or returned, she walks me right to the cabinet above her little cat tree to remind me where the cat food can be found (glancing back to confirm my compliance and vocalizing what is apparently a hunger-induced rant about my negligence). She doesn't rub along my arm or purr in anticipation—not to be mean I don't think, but it is her response to the current mood! Instead, she glares silently, sitting like a little, blue Egyptian cat statue you might uncover during the excavation of an Alexandria archaeological site from 1450 B.C. She stares at the food being portioned onto the plate, and without an acknowledgement, she eats with her normal elegance.

She is at least annoyed, but I don't think mad—and she recovers quickly back to being herself. That's how she taught me to be more forgiving. See, too often those little annoyances, disruptions, or things happening just a bit not like I plan can cause me to become irritated or annoyed. But Killer reacts to similar disturbances in her life with a "shake-it-off" attitude, and that is the notion behind being more forgiving: not letting the little things that are of no consequence (or even some bigger things that still have insignificant consequence) get in the way. Maybe for us it's when someone cuts us off in a work meeting or when a server makes a mistake with a meal at a restaurant. It's these little transgressions that we seem to put so much weight on that they add up in a day to a real burden for us. Thank goodness Killer was so readily forgiving that I learned how refreshing it can feel, too!

~

It's hard for me sometimes to let my brain process that Killer is not just another human family member. She's with me all the time, I shop for her, I make her bed, and I tend to her water fountain when it needs cleaned. But, more than that administrative work of owning a cat, I spend time with her, play with her, and do the many fun and engaging things with her about which you have already read. So, when I leave her, I think about her a lot, and I've caught myself with a little guilt over it—so that's why I asked Kimber to be her cat sitter, and it's why I got her a couple of little sometimes playmates. Now, that guilt is pretty easy to set aside; see, I know that I have to go to work, go on vacation, and otherwise leave her for some stretches. That's the kind of forgiving yourself that is not too difficult to do, of course.

However, there are those things that we reflect on—maybe even from years ago—that are more meaningful because they harmed, hurt, or otherwise caused someone else pain. Those are a little more difficult to process for forgiveness when they bubble to your mind.

I'm sure I have at least my fair share of things that I wish I could go back and change to relieve the hurt or pain that I caused with my words or my actions. Often, those weigh on us heavily—and maybe even long after the recipient because they already granted themselves the forgiveness through relief the psychologists suggest for liberation.

Over the last few years, it has become much easier to forgive myself for a lot of the things I can remember, which allows me to instead focus on growth instead of doubt, anger, and disappointment from past behaviors.

It's not just the little things, either, that we have to allow ourselves the freedom from guilt or burden. We overlook and slip-up all the time, and I sometimes give myself way too hard a time for those minor transgressions. Killer taught me to stop that.

She once took a roll of toilet paper and just unrolled it for the fun of it. Now, this is not unique to her—how many of us have walked into the bathroom because we hear the low, rapid whirring of the roll being unfurled along the floor below? I found her mid-swipe, and she looked at me with that knowing look that it was not okay to be doing this little game she must have thought it was. So, she stopped, sat upright and looked at me, rose and walked by me with a rub against the leg, and left. Believe it or not, she never again unrolled the toilet paper. How nice to make a mistake, learn from it, and leave it behind.

~

So, I won't spend another minute thinking about the guilt and remorse I used to carry because I didn't invite him to my high school graduation, and maybe my dad will read this and learn the answer to that question he asked me.

Killer would have told him if he had asked her.

9

Lesson Seven: Love

I had wanted to visit the Canary Islands for a longer time than the one-day stop a cruise I had been on made there several years ago. I was finishing a book about curriculum and assessment (the field in which I work), and I thought that a little balcony overlooking the Atlantic would give me just the uninterrupted time I needed to complete it. It wasn't quite the warmest season there yet, so I figured I would not be distracted by the weather, the beach, or the water.

The flight was a typical overnight flight to Europe from Tampa that didn't depart until almost ten at night, so I spent the day of the flight out front getting the yard cleaned up, trimming some bushy plants, and clearing away a lot of the southern live oak leaves that had landed on the garden beds since last fall. Of course, Killer joined me out there, and we spent most of the day together enjoying the cooler March sun—and her the new ant hills that form endlessly in the cracks of the driveway.

She could watch these ants for hours, it seems. She never attacks them, but she is especially fond of watching them make their trails, build their little mounds, and get just up to her paw before they realized she was something living and turn the other way. Like a spectator at a tennis match, her head looks one way then the other as she watches them go about their day, only occasionally glancing back toward me to see if I am still outside.

On that Friday I was particularly glad to have had the time to spend with her out there, as ten days away from her might have been the longest in almost five years! She wandered down to the end of the driveway a couple of times, which meant that I had to go get her (she had selective hearing), and she even once made her way to the neighbor's yard along the fence where she showed off her roaming freedom to the dogs held in their yard. From time-to-time she investigated what remained of the tree that she used to spend so much time lying under—it had been claimed by Hurricane Ian a few years prior. Otherwise, she and I spent about five hours together outside before we headed in so that I could get ready to head up to Tampa for my flight.

By about five in the afternoon, the little ones and Killer were ready for dinner, and I added a few sardines onto their plates that night as a special treat because I knew that Melayna would not dare touch them while I was away. Killer didn't often have sardines, so she was always a bit surprised when she saw them lying alongside her seafood pâté. In fact, I'm not sure she knew they were not alive, as she batted them a few times before convincing herself they were part of the feast. After Killer performed a little grooming and took a short nap, I played a little laser with her, brushed her to pull off whatever loose hairs she missed, and then reassured her I would see her in just a "little while," which I had begun to believe she understood and gave her solace she was not being abandoned for long.

~

The first flight to Zurich was uneventful, and we landed in the late morning hours of Saturday. It was quiet, as the skiing season was ending, and the summer travel season would not begin for several more weeks. I only had a connection here, anyway, so I grabbed a bite (apparently baguettes with plain ham are all the rage at Zurich airport) and waited for my flight with coffee and a quick FaceTime call back home just to check how things were. Melayna was a little alarmed because Killer had had an accident on the bedroom floor where she had her bed, which is very unusual for a cat because they ordinarily would go to great lengths to keep their sleeping and eating areas clean. At any rate, I told her that maybe it was just a little one-off thing and boarded my flight to the islands shortly after that.

~

Killer loves her bedroom that she also lets Melayna use! She has a little pink "cuddler" bed, her form-fitting scratcher bed, and a ribbon-shaped Hello Kitty velvet bench that she rarely sleeps on but instead uses exclusively to hop onto Melayna's bed. I mentioned earlier that Killer sleeps a little bit less in my room at night because the little ones annoy her in there, and she has begun to spend more time overnight in Melayna's room. It works out for both of them, as Melayna enjoys the company as much as Killer does, and she still has a nice big lanai slider to take in the late morning sun.

I think Melayna does a lot for Killer from the perspective of comfort and security. The little ones recognized early that Melayna's room was not for them, and Killer started to feel a real comfort with Melayna because the other cats engage less with her. See, Melayna worked and went to school, so a lot of her time was quiet time—studying, listening to music, relaxing with friends—while I am in the garage doing woodworking, outside working on the yard, remodeling, or otherwise doing stuff that just makes more noise! Killer likes the calm environment that Melayna provides for her.

~

By about 5:30 pm I was in my room at the resort, and it was as nice as I expected. I was confident that I would be able to focus on the book and have something to send to the editor when I returned a little over a week later. A large balcony extended from one bedroom, across the living area, and then across the other bedroom. There were two seating areas on the balcony, as well as an area to lie back and enjoy the sun and breeze that blew in from the Atlantic about fifty feet below. I set up my workspace and then headed into Maspalomas to find some food at Yumba Centrum, which is the center of live music, food, shopping, and other activities on the island, including, this week, Carnival. I realized quickly that if I were to participate in a lot of the activity, I would have to nap more and work less—the place really didn't come alive until after 9:00 pm, and most folks didn't leave until after 3 am! I resigned to visiting another time for that because I really did have a focus on this trip.

~

By midmorning Sunday I was well into carefully proofreading the completed chapters—the technical nature of that text meant that I had to hold strict to all the rules of writing! I had hoped by midafternoon I could move on to writing the remaining chapters that had only been sketched out. Around noon, Melayna called and wanted to let me know that Killer had again used the bedroom floor overnight and again during the day, so I was a little more concerned now because this was a new dynamic even for a cat that has some history in this area.

I had taken Killer to the vet a few weeks before because that's what I do every time I hear a sniffle, see her behave differently than normal for more than five minutes, or in some way give an indication that I interpret as illness. (My previous vet had instituted a requirement that I call her first before I came in, as she felt guilty financing her vacations with my uncertainties.) The visit ended with a little paste to add to her meal to get everything inside working better, and she did appear a little better by the end of that week.

Now, however, I thought that there might be more going on and asked Melayna to take her to the veterinary hospital down in Port Charlotte just to be sure. She and her friends were shopping up in Sarasota, but they went home and tricked her into the crate around 7 pm to head off to the hospital.

There was a bit of a wait at the hospital, but the girls appreciated that it would be busy on a Sunday evening and used the time to catch-up, scroll social media, and relax outside on the benches the hospital has out front. By 9 pm, Killer was in the exam room, examined, and I was on the phone with the vet listening to some ideas and recommendations. She recommended an x-ray or ultrasound along with some standard bloodwork, which I agreed to even knowing the cost was going to be crazy compared to the regular vet the next day. But, given that she had just been to the vet and her behavior was unusual, I asked them to go ahead and do the imaging and testing because we were all ready to find out what was going on.

Melayna called me at about 5 am Canary Island time to ask me if I would talk directly to the doctor. Of course! I was ready to hear that Killer has a little infection or something that was bothering her and that getting her to take an antibiotic for the next seven days was our next challenge.

As I think about it now, I am not exactly sure what I heard when the vet talked to me about the radiologist's interpretation of Killer's x-ray the first time she summarized it for me. When she repeated it, however, I was able to process quickly enough that Killer has a spinal cancer that has spread to her lungs, and I already knew what I would hear next.

~

Over the few weeks before I left, I paid little attention to the fact that her new favorite spot had become a bed in the corner of my room that I was so excited to buy her years before, but that she shunned for the cardboard scratchers lying around the house—each of which I moved by the season to be sure to get the best direct hit by the sun through the windows. The bed was dark blue like her sometimes eyes, which also could be green, gray, or almost yellow, and it gave her plenty of space to spread out and relax. I originally bought it because it seemed royal enough for her epicurean personality—it was a blue velvet exterior with a gray velvet interior with hand-stitching—and it was right-sized for her mature, rotund, well-nourished but happy body. It was in the far corner of my bedroom shielded on three sides by a dresser, a nightstand, and a wall.

Of course, now I know that she was isolating to protect herself from predators that she didn't know would never come, but from which she was programmed to protect herself when she knew she was sick. The accidents were surely because of pain that she was experiencing stepping into the litter box. How I wish I had seen a first sign before she felt it.

~

Melayna signed the paperwork over the next several minutes, they described to all of us what to expect, and her friends balanced an iPhone against the wall so that I could be with Killer. The decision was not difficult because I had spent five years making sure she was happy, and I would not even let five minutes go by knowing there was a suffering I could save her from. I called out to her by her nickname—the one I told you earlier that only I used—and she turned toward the direction of the screen. I will never not believe that she thought anything other than that I was there comforting her as her eyes closed and she quietly went onto whatever number life was next for her with Melayna stroking her thick fur.

~

As busy as I was on that Friday, I knew that a day outside for her would bring her enjoyment. I never knew how much it would mean for me.

~

I learned a lot about myself through my experiences with Killer. While I fully understand that there is infinitely more to the nuances and dynamics of human relationships, isn't there a lot that is the same, too?

I have elaborated on so much that I learned by watching and taking care of her. I only wish I could go on to share more. But let me mention just a few more things I didn't get to before I wrap up her story—things I want to offer family, friends, and even co-workers or strangers because I learned them better from Killer. In no particular order—I'll continue to fit all of them into the right situation for me when I can—are a few thoughts as Killer would want me to remember.

Take time to acknowledge. Killer did so easily—a purr, a rub across the calf to express dedication, or even a meow to greet me at the door. Simple gestures such as these were her way to say, "You are important to me," and I can offer them easily, too: a simple thank-you to a co-worker for doing something they're expected to do anyway, a hello to the cashier instead of continuing that conversation into my ear buds, or a quick conversation while waiting in line at the post office All of these are pretty easy ways to offer someone else a moment of kindness and humanity.

Give consistency. Killer hopped into bed every night, watched TV at my feet, and yielded her whatever-she-was-doing time to me when I came home from a long trip. Such unbroken constants in my life reassure, build a sense of trust and comfort, and remind me of the special nature of a relationship. The absence of erratic and irregular behavior that I was witness to with Killer helped me to see personal deficiencies that I am more careful to be mindful of today.

Listen to understand—not just to respond. A change in the pitch of Killer's meow, a slight rumble from deeper in her throat, or a little cadence change in her purr helped me to prioritize the importance of listening to understand. If I hadn't, the request for a treat might have gotten Killer a trip to the vet! Too often, I prepare a response just as another begins speaking, and I surely cannot comprehend, consider, or appreciate what was said if I have already decided my next words. Especially when others feel hurt or marginalized, it is important that I listen with empathy for meaning and context.

Encourage. Killer prodded the little ones to jump higher and run faster during those times they played together. It was an encouragement of sorts to them—learn your limit! And didn't she encourage me just the same by making visible what I hadn't seen before her? I have committed to finding more ways to encourage others and myself since I watched that, and it has been inspiring to me and the beneficiaries.

~

Our last day together was like any other as it started. Breakfast, coffee on the lanai, hunting a lizard or two (her, not me). But, as the sun rose higher, she hinted at some front yard time with a soft purr at the front door, a few nestles against my legs, and a light scratching on the hinges (she never learned which side opened). And because of those signals, you read that we spent a nice, long span of time outside that morning and early afternoon.

Killer's water bowl was still in the front yard when I returned from my trip about a week after she died. I picked it up on the way in the house—row after row of salt lines marking the stopping point of the water's evaporation of each day in the Florida sun. As a scientist, I noted the evidence it provided about how fast water evaporated or how hot it might have been each day: was there a band that was farther spaced from another? And as a scientist, I never look for *proof*—just evidence of a truth. I walked into the house for the first time without Killer greeting me, and everything she helped me to make more important was revealed without her now. I contemplated what it provided evidence of.

~

I set the bowl down on the coffee table I built around Christmastime a few years ago. Remember, Killer taught me to take chances in the world, and this table was here because her life intersected with mine. I watched her thrive once she was out from behind that old dining room window, and so I followed her lead. I was living a set of experiences that I wanted to know since I first smelled the burning wood and sawdust in a garage almost forty years before.

Once I was settled, I wanted to go through who called and left messages on my phone, which I had decided to put aside while I was working on my book. All those names—family and friends alike! Names that might not have been there even just two years ago if Killer had not caused me to think about the importance of *today*—and not instead of the mistakes of some yesterdays, the essence of which we probably had long forgotten but that kept friends or family apart anyway. Guilt, anger, regret are certainly burdens too heavy; I would rather my strength be used on growing and learning than holding on to those weights.

I reflected on our Friday morning outside together as I carried the bowl into the kitchen. Even knowing how demanding it was to have to run to the grass line along the street's edge to grab her when she got too close, the patience she showed with me and when the little ones came along allowed me to build it better into myself. So even though I knew that day would be busy, I dealt with the number of times I would have to go get her and took her out for one of her longest front yard trips ever. How thankful I am for that decision today.

The little ones had already come into the living room when the squeak of the front door told them somebody was back, and they spent awhile telling me about their week in all kinds of words for which they must have meaning. It was their way of acknowledging my importance to them, which is one of those expectations and needs that Killer highlighted as part of a close, intimate relationship. We played a little feather and laser, and it was not unexpected to see them look around for Killer, as they almost always accepted being spectators until Killer tired of the light.

Melayna heard us and came out of her room where she had been catching a quick nap before work. I realized then that even in my grief, she needed comfort, as well—I lost my cat, but we both lost a friend. The hugs we gave each other were no different to us than Killer's Nike boxes were to her.

Later, I crawled into bed, and of course I was keenly aware that Sir Isaac Newton's protégé was not performing her nighttime calculations. I thought of the ways in which we had grown together, and I thought a lot about the mistakes I may have made—I mean, she was my first cat. How mad I must have made her at times not knowing she wanted to be higher than the counter allowed or that she wanted something to scratch in *every* room. What a disaster she must have thought this was going to be when I first gave her water in a bowl instead of a fountain! And I suppose she thought it an unforgiveable affront that I should bring more cats into her home.

And I stopped there. No. It was not unforgiveable—maybe nothing was for her. She reminded me after every mistake that forgiveness was not only available but readily given with a nudge of her nose for a scratch, a purr when running to the door, or a head on my lap on the couch. This was maybe the most important lesson she taught me.

~

And so I fell asleep thinking about her glance into the iPhone in her last few moments. Those were not the eyes of disappointment that I was not there—I mean, she had urged me through example to get out there and do the things I had long wanted, didn't she? Maybe they were the eyes of gratitude for helping her to feel better when the cancer was causing such pain? Maybe her eyes displayed comfort because she believed that I *was* there—and she certainly felt Melayna's touch on her fur? Maybe hers just then were the eyes of grace thanking me for all I had done for her in her short life? Or maybe they were eyes revealing contentment knowing that her job was accomplished in her lessons for me?

The answer to all those questions is yes. It was all of that. Captured in a single moment, her eyes said all she wanted to be sure I knew. Those eyes—still vibrant and dazzling—were all the evidence I needed of the truth that she loved and felt loved.

10

Lesson Eight: Gratitude

I'm not sure if cats really have nine lives, but I know that I had an enriched one because of Killer. She caused me to think about a lot of important things that I had set aside, played down, or ignored—or that I just needed to get better at. I kind of hope she does have more lives—she has a lot to teach, and I would love that she has the chance to do it all over again for someone else.

I don't believe that Killer knew all that she taught me. I mean, of course I don't believe that she knew I was learning something from her—she was a cat, after all. A few days after

Killer died Jamie sent me a cute little video he scrolled upon on Instagram. The words overlayed on the background video of scenes from a cat's life read, *"For us, they are a short part of our lives; for them, we are everything they will ever know."* I think Killer is a much longer part of my life than the author of that knows.

~

There's a quote that starts this book–it's right before the prologue in case you missed it. I was in a place in my life where I was ready to look around more and see things that I maybe I had not spent enough time thinking about, giving to others or myself, or sharing with friends and family. I was glad to have finally reached that point in my life, and it has provided me the opportunity for exciting new things–actually even some things that were kind of really there all along–to get more notice. Killer opened my eyes to that when I watched her simply do what a cat does.

I discovered a lot about creating paths for myself, paths to others, and enabling paths from others in the time since that red book popped up on our first night in the new house.

But, discovering that took a little help…and even a little helper.

Thank you, Killer.

Epilogue

Silverado and Nightmare looked for Killer in a few of her regular spots for some time after she was gone.

Silverado seemed especially to be awaiting her return for a few weeks. For a while, he positioned himself on the foot of my bed around 7:45 in the morning to watch for Killer's appearance in the hallway. When she didn't come to announce breakfast should be prepared, he settled back onto his new Pusheen blanket about fifteen minutes after her expected arrival.

Nightmare has taken the role of keeping Killer's scratchers warm for her in the event she finds her way home—see, there were a couple that Nightmare just knew belonged to Killer and using them would be a red line that should not be crossed. She used them now, including giving them a good scratch before lying down.

I suspect that by now they don't expect to see her coming through the door. My heart tells me they miss her just the same as I do—

maybe they even learned a little bit from her, too.

~

To wrap up, let me return to that third name T.S. Eliot reminds us that all cats have—you remember, that one we will never know because it's known only to her. Here's my take. It turns out it's not a name at all—what it is reveals itself through our shared experiences and how we react to those with each other. It's a set of feelings and emotions that let us *see* whatever it is that this name symbolizes.

For Killer and me, it was that contentment of sitting together on the couch or the playfulness of feeling like kids with just a feather toy. It was accepting that there were times we wanted our own space or that she trusted me enough to express her needs knowing they would be met. It was letting her outside so that she could live bigger and providing her velvet-lined beds because she was special. See, the third name is just a metaphor for the intimacy, bond, and friendship we all can share with mutual understanding, faithfulness, compassion, and sacrifice that truly taking care of one another requires. It's beautiful when it is revealed, and I'm learning better now that it exists for more than just cats. See, we all have a third name we just want someone to know.

Made in the USA
Columbia, SC
29 June 2025

60027990R00085